CONTENTS

Ships in Focus Publications

Correspondence and editorial:
Roy Fenton
18 Durrington Avenue
London SW20 8NT
0181 879 3527
rfenton@rfenton.demon.co.uk

Orders and photographic:
John & Marion Clarkson
18 Franklands, Longton
Preston PR4 5PD
01772 612855

Printed by Amadeus Press Ltd.,
Huddersfield.
Designed by Hugh Smallwood,
John Clarkson and Roy Fenton.
SHIPS IN FOCUS RECORD
ISBN 1 901703 01 0

SHIPS IN FOCUS RECORD 7

This issue sees two tempora
content of previous issues.
format as *Fleet in Focus* w
Record, but for this issue we
group of vessels it featu
interesting, but in no way
Secondly, there is no article on sa... ....
with another biography of a sailing ship in *Record* 8. Our
editorial policy is to cover almost all aspects of shipping history,
at least from the time people began photographing ships in
serious numbers. With such a wide field, it is impossible to cover
all areas in any one issue. We ask those who find their favourite
topic not covered to be patient – over several issues we hope to
give you satisfaction.

What we publish largely depends on what is submitted. At
present we are almost embarrassed by articles on hand or
promised: enough to fill at least three issues. However, more are
welcome, and especially those on topics not well covered –
coastal sail and both deep-sea and coastal passenger ships.
Submissions for the *Fleet in Focus* feature are also welcome. The
fleet must be of a size which can be covered photographically in
one or possibly two issues, and should not have been featured in
an illustrated article or book in recent years. As always a
reasonable amount of help can be given with research or finding
photographs.

Roy Fenton   John Clarkson
                    October 1998

SUBSCRIPTION RATES FOR THREE ISSUES
Subscribers make a saving on the postage of three issues, and
receive each *Record* just as soon as it is published. They are
also eligible for concessions on newly-published *Ships in
Focus* titles. Readers can start their subscription with *any* issue,
and are welcome to backdate it to receive previous issues.

UK	£20	–
Europe (airmail)	£22	–
Rest of world (surface mail)	£22	US$36
Rest of world (airmail)	£30	US$49

Alliance & Dublin's GLENCREE in the Mersey: see page 146.

DUISBURG (top)
Flensburger Schiffbau-Gesellschaft, Flensburg, Germany; 1900, 5,155gt, 388 feet
DUISBURG is seen against a classic background at Cape Town – work by photographer Martin Leendertz which helped spark the editor's interest in these two-funnelled vessels. In Germany at the start of the First World War and with no prospect of trading, DUISBURG was sold in 1915 to G.J.H. Siemers who renamed her BURGERMEISTER VON MELLE, although she seems to have remained in Hamburg.

In March 1920 she was delivered to the French as war reparations and, perhaps surprisingly, she traded under her German name for a period. In 1922 she became MONT AIGOUAL for a Marseilles owner, but was broken up in Toulon in 1924. *[Martin Leendertz, Roy Fenton collection]*

KIEL (bottom)
Flensburger Schiffbau-Gesellschaft, Flensburg, Germany; 1900, 5,143gt, 388 feet
Photographed at Burnie, KIEL had the longest, if not the most active, life of any of the DADG *Zweischornsteiners*. She was at Wilmington in the USA in August 1914, and followed the familiar route of internment succeeded by requisition in April 1917, when she became CAMDEN. In August 1917 she passed from the United States Shipping Board to the US Navy who used her as a transport until February 1919 when she became a submarine depot ship. She served in the Second World War as an accommodation ship, and was broken up at Baltimore in 1949. *[Peter Newall collection]*

TWO-FUNNEL CARGO LINERS
Part One

A second funnel on a cargo ship: technical necessity or mere frippery? What started as the former almost certainly developed into the latter. A general arrangement drawing of ARTESIA, built by Flensburger Schiffbau-Gesellschaft in 1891 shows flues from both ends of the boilers, each leading to their own funnnel. The extra funnel improved draughting arrangements, and was considered necessary when extra speed was needed. But with the twentieth century, and particularly the arrival of the motorship, the extra funnels placed on a few cargo ships were intended more to impress, as was clearly the case on many passenger ships. Indeed, the last example to be fitted was quite obviously a dummy. This two-part feature looks at the relatively small but fascinating group of cargo liners which were built with two funnels.

Defining terms

Although we are anxious for feedback on this article, to avoid unnecessary correspondence it is as well to define what we mean by two funnels and by cargo liner. We have restricted consideration here to two funnels in line astern; a number of cargo liners were built around the sixties with twin exhausts abreast, but these do not feature here, which is not to say an article on them would be unwelcome. By cargo liner we mean a ship built for a regular route but with very limited passenger accommodation. For British ships, this tended to be for no more than twelve passengers, but on US routes, particularly, ships which were obviously cargo carriers accommodated somewhat more than this. We are aware that at least four tankers and a large number of cross channel steamers, tugs, cable ships and icebreakers had two funnels, but these too are ineligible. We have also turned our back on multi-funnel vessels designed as liners but completed in wartime as pure cargo carriers or which ended their days with their accommodation unused, and - perhaps oddest of all - the seven multi-funnel US destroyers which were employed as banana carriers after the First World War. Ships designed and built essentially as cargo liners give us plenty to cover, although we have allowed in some delightful little ships which are, strictly speaking, fruiters.

From Blue Funnel to dummy funnel

The first two-funnel cargo liner we can trace is Alfred Holt's STENTOR (2,021/1875) built by Scott and Co., Greenock as the first of a class of five, although TEUCER (2,057/1877) had just one funnel. A photograph of STENTOR is included in *Ships in Focus: Blue Funnel Line*, published simultaneously with this issue of *Record*. The oldest two-funneller illustrated here is the PRINCIPIA of 1881.

Although Houlder Brothers built two well-known examples in 1890 and 1891, the most familiar examples of this type were German, the *Zweischornsteiners* built mostly at Flensburg. The first Flensburg-built example known to us is the ARTESIA (2,813/1891) completed for Hamburg-Pacific-Dampschiffs Linie A.G., Hamburg. She had a tragically short life, and on 17th June 1892 stranded at Passage Point in the Magellan Straits whilst on a voyage from Corral and Valparaiso to Hamburg with nitrate and general cargo, sinking the next day. We believe we have illustrated all the other German examples, with the exception of LAEISZ (5,157/1901) built for Deutsche Australisch D.G. but wrecked in the Red Sea on 16th March 1908 whilst bound from Sydney to Antwerp with general cargo.

The need for speed in the US fruit trades probably decided Burmeister & Wain of Copenhagen to fit two funnels to some of the neat banana carriers it built in the early years of this century. But, with subsequent examples of two-funnellers, the extra stack was probably there to impress. Charles Dunn of Liverpool was probably trying to make an impression on his charterers with the HOWICK HALL and CROFTON HALL, and this was certainly the aim with the ill-fated Norwegian motorships SUD-EXPRESSO and SUD-AMERICANO. The last examples of the genre, two turbine steamers built for Silver Line just after the Second World War, made no pretence that their extra funnel was real: the dummy being situated too far forward and actually containing some accommodation.

Photographic evidence

The only way to identify two-funnellers is through photographs and illustrations: *Lloyds Registers* do not give them any special labelling. Although a number of people have scoured their photographic archives to find such ships for this feature, it is likely that some have been missed. If anyone knows of any other two-funnel cargo liners falling into our definition above we would be pleased to hear from them, especially if a photograph can be provided.

This compilation has been a team effort, and thanks go to John Bartlett who looked through his collection of illustrations; David Burrell for the Dunn ships; Lawrence Dunn who stimulated the hunt for two-funnellers with his painting of HOWICK HALL and who drew attention to others; John B. Hill and Dennis Johnzon for information on Houlder ships; Arnold Kludas and Reinhardt Schmelzkopf for photographs; Peter Newall who found ships we were unaware of; Bill Schell for the US angle; and Soren Thorsoe for data on Danish-built fruiters.

EARLY BRITISH TWO-FUNNELLERS

PRINCIPIA

Palmers' Shipbuilding and Iron Co. Ltd., Jarrow-on-Tyne; 1881, 2,749gt, 317 feet

It is unclear whether the PRINCIPIA was a tramp or a cargo liner, although it is possible she was both in her time. She was built for the Steamship Principia Co. Ltd., and managed by Newton Brothers and Co. of London. In 1892 they sold her to the Arrow Steamship Co. Ltd., managed in Newcastle-upon-Tyne by Dent and Co.

It would be interesting to know where this photograph was taken, and quite what is being protected on the quayside by the elaborate canvas covers, on which the stevedores are standing.

PRINCIPIA and Dent's other steamers ran from time to time on sailings of the Arrow Line from British east coast ports to New York. It was on such a sailing, from Dundee with general cargo, that PRINCIPIA was lost on 28th November 1895. Fire broke out when she was 110 miles north of Cape Wrath, and in attempting to run for the Faroes she struck a rock and sank. *[Peter Newall collection]*

MONKSEATON

C.S. Swan and Hunter, Newcastle-upon-Tyne, 1882, 2,713gt, 326 feet

Built for Elliot, Lowrey and Dunford of Newcastle-upon-Tyne, the iron steamer MONKSEATON was probably intended for the tramp trades. Like many contemporaries, she originally had two-cylinder compound engines, built in her case by R. and W. Hawthorn, and these were tripled in 1893. This extended her life, and in 1907 her owners – by now just Dunford and Elliot – sold her to Italy where she was broken up in July 1908. She is seen here at Barrow-in-Furness.
[Sankey Collection 768]

NELSON, DONKIN & CO.

BOMBAY

C. Mitchell and Co., Newcastle-upon-Tyne; 1882, 3,133gt, 337 feet

Henry Nelson of Newcastle-upon-Tyne began to build up a fleet of steamers in 1870, and when he took Donkin into partnership in 1873 had a total of seven. Nelson, Donkin and Co. also quickly built up a fleet, perhaps the most impressive of which were BOMBAY and FLORIDA, built locally in 1882. Despite eventually owning 19 ships, little has been recorded about the company's operations, but from the geographical distribution of its several losses it can be assumed the ships were tramping or on charter to liner operators. It is known that the BOMBAY's sister FLORIDA sailed from Liverpool in November 1886 for the Huntington Line, a short-lived transAtlantic service connected with the Newport News and Mississippi Valley Railroad.

In 1909, BOMBAY was sold to Chr. Christensen of Sandefjord who used her for whaling operations. Not until 1922 was she renamed PROFESSOR GRUVEL. On 12th October 1927 the now-elderly ship foundered after striking ice some 600 miles south of the Falklands. *[National Maritime Museum G1933]*

FLORIDA

C. Mitchell and Co., Newcastle-upon-Tyne; 1882, 3,202gt, 337 feet

BOMBAY's sister FLORIDA had a very similar career, being sold to the same Norwegian whalers in 1908, and renamed ORN. She changed hands in 1913, becoming FALKLAND, but was wrecked off Montevideo on 12th November of that year. *[National Maritime Museum P10324]*

HOULDER LINERS

HORNBY GRANGE (top)
Wigham, Richardson and Co., Newcastle-upon-Tyne; 1890, 2,473gt, 300 feet
HORNBY GRANGE was the first steamer owned by Houlder Brothers, and her name began with the 'H' of 'Houlder', initiating the tradition of using names beginning with one of the letters of the title 'Houlder Brothers'. Houlders were deeply involved with the carriage of meat from South America and Australia, and HORNBY GRANGE had 70,000 cubic feet of refrigerated space. Some views of the ship show that she crossed three yards on her foremast, but these are gone by the time of this view. In 1919 - after 29 years with Houlders – she was sold to owners in Valencia and renamed AUGUSTINA FORNER, as which she was broken up at Barcelona in 1927.

OVINGDEAN GRANGE (bottom)
Raylton, Dixon and Co., Middlesbrough; 1890, 2,413gt, 297 feet
A contemporary of HORNBY GRANGE, and built to similar design, OVINGDEAN GRANGE nevertheless shows some detail differences, including taller funnels. She was sold in 1907 to Russian owners and renamed ROMAN, being sold on to Japan in 1915 to become TAMON MARU No. 16. She passed Woosung on 7th September 1917 whilst on a voyage from Hanyang to Wakamatsu loaded with pig iron and was never seen again.

BUTESHIRE (opposite top) and BOLLINGTON GRANGE (opposite middle)
Hawthorn, Leslie and Co., Hebburn-on-Tyne; 1893, 5,583gt, 420 feet
Amongst the rarefied group of two-funnellers, BUTESHIRE was unique in having funnels of unequal size. BUTESHIRE was the second of a pair of ships built on Tyneside in 1893 for Turnbull, Martin's Elderslie Steamship Co. Ltd. – forerunner of the Scottish Shire Line. Although both BUTESHIRE and PERTHSHIRE were built to the same set of plans, these do not show the forward, smaller diameter funnel.

Dennis Johnzon researched the BUTESHIRE extensively in the 1980s, and published a detailed article on her which speculated that the odd funnel might have been intended to serve the refrigeration machinery. Soon afterwards he learned the real reason from Captain E.E. Sigwart, from whose collection come this and many other photographs in this feature. PERTHSHIRE (5,550/1893) was bought by the Admiralty in 1914 and served in various roles, including masquerading as the battleship HMS VANGUARD. She rapidly moved down the social scale, however, becoming the coaling officer's ship at Scapa Flow and later a hulk at Malta. In her final role she was refitted for service with the Royal Fleet Auxiliary and her last master was Captain Sigwart. He explained that the PERTHSHIRE had been built with the stove pipe for the donkey boiler clamped to her funnel. The owners had thought this was ugly, and in near-sister BUTESHIRE the stovepipe was made altogether heftier, almost the size of a funnel, in fact.

As Dennis relates in his article, BUTESHIRE had a fascinating career.

Turnbull Martin were loosely associated with Houlder Brothers, and in conjunction with Federal Line they operated a joint service of refrigerated steamers from the United Kingdom to Australia and New Zealand. In 1915 Houlders bought BUTESHIRE and renamed her BOLLINGTON GRANGE (the 'B' taken from 'Brothers'), but in 1916 she was transferred to the newly-formed Furness-Houlder Argentine Line and became CANONESA. Of three attacks by submarines she suffered, by far the worst was on 1st May 1918 when torpedoed by UB 57 in the English Channel south of Worthing. Eight lives were lost, and a bizarre result of the torpedo explosion was that one of the lifeboats was blown into the air and ended up perched on top of the after funnel. The other boats were launched, but CANONESA remained afloat and was brought into Southampton Water. Here she was abandoned to the British Government, as war loss insurers. She was bought by the Blue Star Line Ltd. and rebuilt, losing her forward 'funnel' to become MAGICSTAR. She was broken up at Inverkeithing in 1930. *[Peter Newall collection and George Scott collection]*

REBUILD

HONG MOH (opposite bottom)
Charles Connell and Co., Glasgow; 1881, 3,954gt, 400 feet
This is not an early example of a ship having two funnels: she was built with only one. She was completed as the third CITY OF CALCUTTA for George Smith and Sons of Glasgow, who later restyled themselves City Line. When the company was sold to John Ellerman in 1901, soon after the death of its founder, the three-masted iron steamer with obsolete two-cylinder engines was sold to a Singapore owner and renamed HONG MOH. Her engines were tripled by the Hong Kong and Whampoa Dock Co. Ltd. in 1916, and this must be when she lost a mast and gained a funnel. This rebuilding might have been

forced on her owners by an incident on 5th January 1916 when HONG MOH struck a mine laid off Aden by the German commerce raider WOLF. HONG MOH survived under the ownership of Ho Hong Steamship Co. Ltd. of Singapore for only a few years longer, and was wrecked off Swatow on 3rd March 1921 whilst on a voyage from Singapore to Amoy. *[Peter Newall collection]*

ZWEISCHORNSTEINERS

MEISSEN (top) and **HERSFELD** (middle)
*Flensburger Schiffbau-Gesellschaft,
Flensburg, Germany; 1897, 5,150gt, 388 feet*
Germany built more two-funnellers than anyone else, all but two coming from the Flensburger yard. The first is believed to be ARTESIA, completed in April 1891 for Hamburg-Pacific-Dampschiffs Linie A.G., Hamburg. Between 1897 and 1901 the Flensburg builders turned out a series of 13 for Deutsche Australisch D.G.(DADG), establishing a very distinctive appearance for this fleet.

The first DADG *Zweischornsteiner* was MEISSEN, seen here in Australian or New Zealand waters. In 1913 she was sold to H.H. Schmidt of Hamburg who renamed her WOGLINDE, and in 1916 she became HERSFELD. She would see little more than local service under these names, and was taken as a prize by the UK in May 1919, being placed under the management of F.C. Strick and Co. by The Shipping Controller. The middle photograph may show her actually being delivered, the legend 'Waffenstillstande Armistice' being painted on her hull. She reverted to German ownership as RUTH KAYSER in 1921, but in 1926 returned to the UK for the final time and was broken up at Bo'ness. *[Both: Peter Newall collection]*

BIELEFELD (bottom)
*Flensburger Schiffbau-Gesellschaft,
Flensburg, Germany; 1898, 5,104gt, 388 feet*
A sister of MEISSEN, BIELEFELD had a more active war than most of her running mates, being taken over by the Kaiserlichen Marine immediately on the outbreak of war and renamed first SPERRBRECHER 3 and from 1915 SPERRBRECHER 5. Sperrbrecher translates as 'barrier-breaker' and she was presumably engaged in her new profession of blockade running on 22nd June 1915 when torpedoed by a British submarine off Juist - the Germans obviously not having a monopoly of trying to sink merchant ships. SPERRBRECHER 5 made it into Hamburg

and was repaired, and returned to her owners as BIELEFELD. The British finally got her in April 1919 when she became a war prize, but she was awarded to Japan whose Department of Finance renamed her KOBIN MARU in 1920. Under this name she was lost east of Shanghai on 29th December 1928 whilst on a voyage from Japan to Singapore. *[Sammlung Verfasser, courtesy Reinhart Schmelzkopf]*

ELBING (top)
*Flensburger Schiffbau-Gesellschaft,
Flensburg, Germany; 1898, 5,587gt, 404 feet*
Deutsche Australisch D.G. had their two-funnellers built to two different lengths, and ELBING was the first of the larger version. In this view the canvas used to maximise the effect of the engine room ventilator can be seen.

ELBING was in Antwerp on the outbreak of war in August 1914, and seems to have remained there until the British Shipping Controller took possession of her as a prize in April 1919. Again, she soon returned to Germany, as HEINRICH KAYSER for Reederei Kayser AG of Hamburg. Her subsequent career was short. On 2nd December 1922 she sailed from Norfolk, Virginia with coal for Bremen but the last that was heard from her was an SOS sent out on 6th December. *[Arnold Kludas collection]*

VARZIN (middle)
*Flensburger Schiffbau-Gesellschaft,
Flensburg, Germany; 1899, 5,192gt, 388 feet*
An earlier view of VARZIN shows that she originally crossed a yard arm just above the prominent crow's nest on her foremast. VARZIN was one of many German ships at sea when war broke out in August 1914, and was captured by the Royal Navy off Aden on 13th August. The Admiralty made their own use of ships they captured, although they placed her management with Grahams and Co. of London without renaming her. In 1919 owners became the Secretary of State for India. In 1922 she was sold to Greek owners who gave her the names ELECTRA STAVROUDI and IOANNIS TH VLASSOPOULOS before she was broken up at Genoa in 1929. *[Peter Newall collection]*

HARBURG (bottom)
*Flensburger Schiffbau-Gesellschaft,
Flensburg, Germany; 1899; 5,134gt, 388 feet*
HARBURG was in New York in 1914, and remained there until the USA entered the First World War when, on 6th April 1917, she was taken over by the United States Shipping Board and renamed PAWNEE. After neglect and some disabling of the machinery by the crew, such prizes were of doubtful value, but PAWNEE did find a post-war buyer, the California Steam Ship Co., which found it convenient to register her in Panama in 1922. She was broken up in Hong Kong in 1928. *[Sammlung Verfasser, courtesy Reinhart Schmelzkopf]*

ZWEISCHORNSTEINERS (continued)

ITZEHOE (top and second down)
Flensburger Schiffbau-Gesellschaft,
Flensburg, Germany; 1899, 5,134gt, 388 feet
In the upper photograph, ITZEHOE has DADG's coastal steamer TECK (577/1891) alongside. On 24th May 1911 ITZEHOE was on a voyage from Hamburg to Australia with general cargo when she stranded at Cap Recife, as seen in the second photograph. *[World Ship Photo Library and Peter Newall collection]*

BERGEDORF (third down)
Sir Raylton Dixon and Co. Ltd.,
Middlesbrough; 1900, 5,125gt, 390 feet
Surprisingly, the sequence of *Zweischornsteiners* built at Flensburg was broken by one from a Britsh yard. Seen here at Amsterdam in March 1901, BERGEDORF is practically indistinguishable from the Flensburg-built vessels, and it must be assumed that the same plans were used, possibly because the German yard was fully committed. BERGEDORF had a relatively short life. On 4th April 1911 she stranded at Cape Comorin whilst homeward bound from Port Pirie to Hamburg. *[G.J. de Boer]*

MAGDEBURG (bottom)
Flensburger Schiffbau-Gesellschaft,
Flensburg, Germany; 1900, 5,154gt, 388 feet
Short but intense excitement or lengthy inactivity was the lot of German steamers in wartime, and MAGDEBURG experienced the former. In August 1914 she was at Las Palmas and was called upon to take a cargo of coal to the auxiliary cruiser KAISER WILHELM DER GROSSE, which she met between 24th and 26th August. MAGDEBURG then sailed for New York, and internment, which lasted until April 1917 when the United States Shipping Board took her over and gave her the name NEUSE. She was broken up in 1923. *[Reinhart Schmelzkopf]*

APOLDA (top and middle)
Flensburger Schiffbau-Gesellschaft,
Flensburg, Germany; 1901, 4,950gt, 391 feet
The top photograph was taken at Hull,
DADG obviously engaging in the homeward
wool trade from Australia which delivered
the season's wool clip to the Yorkshire
woollen industry.

APOLDA was captured by the British in
August 1914, when arriving at the Cape on a
voyage from Hamburg. The lower
photograph shows her after the war,
working for the South African Railways and
Harbour Administration, but still as APOLDA.
In 1927 she was sold to owners in Genoa,
becoming VERBANIA but, after a period of
lay-up at her home port, was broken up in
1932. *[Middle: Peter Newall collection]*

ROSTOCK (bottom)
Flensburger Schiffbau-Gesellschaft,
Flensburg, Germany; 1901, 4,972gt, 391 feet
ROSTOCK is seen here in the Suez Canal,
which she had the misfortune to be
transiting in August 1914 during a voyage
from Brisbane to Hamburg. Detained at Port
Said on 5th August, she was later
condemned as a war prize. In 1915 she was
renamed HUNTSMOOR, one of the 'Hun'
names which have not been adequately
explained: it seems a bit crass to have
based the names of a whole group of now
British ships on a nickname for the enemy,
but subtlety was something the British
Government could hardly be accused of
during the First World War. HUNTSMOOR
was used initially as a frozen meat ship, but
later designated an Expeditionary Force
Transport. On 20th February 1918
HUNTSMOOR was 23 miles south of the
Owers Light Vessel when torpedoed by UB
40, one of many German submarines
operating from bases in Belgium. *[World
Ship Photo Library]*
*The story of the two-funnel cargo liners will
be concluded in* Record 8

PHOTOGRAPHER IN FOCUS:
JOHN McROBERTS
Craig J. M. Carter

Ship photographer, maritime researcher and writer, John McRoberts of Wallasey, Merseyside had a long association with the Mersey shipping scene, and over the years built up a collection of about 50,000 photographs and transparencies of ships large and small.

Born in 1902 in Belfast, he was very proud of being a Northern Irishman. His father was a chief engineer with the Belfast Steamship Co. Ltd. and for a long period he was chief of their PATRIOTIC operating on the overnight Liverpool-Belfast service.

The McRoberts family moved to Wallasey while John was still a boy and he went to school in Liverpool. On leaving school he joined a firm of Liverpool cotton brokers and, travelling to and from the office each day by the Wallasey ferry, he began to take an interest in photographing the many ships of all types that he saw in the busy Mersey tideway.

Although John never went to sea himself, his brother became a chief engineer with Furness, Withy & Co. Ltd. and this heightened John's interest in ships.

When war broke out in September 1939 John served with an RAF barrage balloon unit, locally at first, before being moved to the South of England.

Upon his return to civilian life John combined his maritime interests with work by joining the staff of the *Journal of Commerce and Shipping Telegraph* in the shipping movements department at its Liverpool head office. For some years his duties took him out along the Liverpool docks, visiting the various dockmaster's offices and collecting details of arrivals, sailings and changes of berths within the dock system. As he carried his camera with him he was presented with many fine opportunities for ship photography. Later he was moved to a different job inside the office, collating ships' movements from all over the world.

For many years John supplied photographs to the Nautical Photo Agency, founded in London by Captain Fred C. Poyser and to various publications, including *Sea Breezes* at that time part of the Journal of Commerce organisation. He became friendly with other ship photographers, notably Alex Duncan of Gravesend and Tom Rayner, of Ryde, Isle of Wight, working closely with Tom exchanging negatives and information.

John continued working in the shipping movements department of the *Journal of Commerce* until his retirement in 1967, continuing to build up his extensive photograph collection. He then set to work

DUNKERY BEACON
Cammell, Laird & Co. Ltd., Birkenhead;
1941, 7,069gt, 432 feet
DUNKERY BEACON began life as EMPIRE FLAME, a Y-type, one of the earliest wartime standard ships, and not prefabricated like most emergency cargo vessels. One of only two such ships built at Birkenhead, she was also unusual in being

converted to a merchant aircraft carrier.

H.G. Mann managed the steamer from 1942, and bought her in 1945, registering her under their Crawford Shipping Co. Ltd. and renaming her DUNKERY BEACON. Although partly obscured by a kingpost in John McRobert's August 1947 view, the company had a colourful funnel with a red

six-pointed star on a white disc, flanked by a white-bordered blue band, all on black. Sadly, this funnel disappeared in 1948 when it was replaced by that of Phs. van Ommeren of Holland who had bought the company. DUNKERY BEACON was sold to Finnish owners in 1955 to become RISSA and, from 1961, AUGUSTA PAULIN. She was broken up at Shanghai in 1969.

researching and writing, completing the detailed histories of several well-known shipping companies for publication in *Sea Breezes*.

A bachelor all his life, after the death of his parents John lived with his sister Margaret, who also never married. Never a man to suffer fools gladly, nevertheless those he counted as his friends were always aware of his readiness to share with them his knowledge of ships and of photography.

John died in Wallasey in July 1982 at the age of 80, leaving most of his library of maritime books and photographic prints to the Merseyside Maritime Museum. He put on record a large section of the Mersey shipping scene and his meticulously researched articles are still referred to by students of maritime history.

JAMAICA SETTLER (top)
Cammell, Laird and Co. Ltd., Birkenhead; 1910, 7,117gt, 406 feet
JAMAICA SETTLER had only just been sold to the Jamaica Direct Fruit Line Ltd. when John McRoberts photographed her in Langton Dock on 6th April 1929. She was still being prepared and painted for her new role as a fruiter: note the Mersey flats alongside.

She had been built on Merseyside as the HIGHLAND LADDIE for Nelson Line, one of a large group of cargo-passenger ships with which Nelson had launched an assault on Royal Mail Lines' trade. HIGHLAND LADDIE was made redundant by the arrival of Nelson Line's celebrated twin-funnel motor passenger ships. Following the sale, JAMAICA SETTLER's service to Jamaica was not lengthy, however, and the steamer was broken up at Dalmuir in 1935.

BEACONSFIELD (bottom)
Caledon Shipbuilding and Engineering Co. Ltd., Dundee; 1938, 4,783gt, 418 feet.
BEACONSFIELD was a relatively new ship when caught by John McRoberts' camera on 1st July 1939, and was one of the last he photographed before the Second World War. The Watts, Watts ship survived the conflict, and went on to give her owners twenty years' good service. In 1958 she was sold to Hong Kong and took the slightly quirky name TWINHORSE, passing through the hands of several obscure operators before fetching up with Japanese breakers in 1964.

HEROIC (top)
Harland and Wolff Ltd., Belfast; 1906, 2,016gt, 320 feet
John McRobert's interest in cross-channel ships was undoubtedly heightened by his father serving as an engineer with the Belfast Steamship Co. Ltd. Here their HEROIC leaves Canada Dock on 7th July 1928 ready to take on passengers at the Landing Stage.

Together with her sister GRAPHIC, HEROIC had been built by the Belfast company to counter opposition from the Midland Railway's Belfast to Heysham service. However, in typical conservative fashion, those new-fangled turbines were rejected in favour of two sets of quadruple expansion steam engines. Their power enabled the overnight sailings to be speeded up by an hour.

HEROIC was made redundant by the arrival of the ULSTER QUEEN and her sisters in 1929, and was transferred within what was now the Coast Lines group to British and Irish Steam Packet Co. Ltd. As LADY CONNAUGHT she gained an additional albeit dummy funnel, and helped to accelerate the Dublin to Liverpool overnight sailings. Unusually amongst group vessels, she had no further transfers and only one renaming, when she became LONGFORD in 1938. She was broken up at Barrow in 1953.

PATRIOTIC (bottom)
Harland and Wolff Ltd., Belfast; 1912, 2,254gt, 325 feet
PATRIOTIC was essentially a slightly grander version of HEROIC, but to John McRoberts she was particularly significant as being his father's ship for many years. With her two four-cylinder triple expansion engines, she was to be the flagship of the Belfast Steamship Co. Ltd. until displaced by the ULSTER QUEEN and her sisters.

In 1929, PATRIOTIC, with her consorts GRAPHIC and HEROIC, was transferred within the Coast Lines group to the British and Irish Steam Packet Co. Ltd. to run between Liverpool and Dublin. Renamed LADY LEINSTER, her hull was painted grey but she lost her imposing single smokestack in place of two somewhat squat funnels, the after one being a dummy. She was renamed LADY CONNAUGHT in 1938, and was intended to become a cruise ship, but this plan was postponed by the outbreak of war. It was not until June 1947 that she took up this intended role, transferred to Coast Lines Ltd. and renamed LADY KILLARNEY. After a long and varied life she arrived at Port Glasgow on 17th December 1956 to be broken up by Smith and Houston Ltd.

ULSTER QUEEN

Harland and Wolff Ltd., Belfast; 1930, 3,735gt, 340 feet

ULSTER QUEEN was another Belfast passenger ship to be built in the face of railway competition, in this case plans to build new ships for the Heysham service now operated by the London, Midland and Scotttish Railway. The response of the Belfast company was a powerful one, the first cross-channel passenger ships in British services to have oil engines.

ULSTER QUEEN was the second of three, the others being ULSTER MONARCH and ULSTER PRINCE.

The service the company obtained from the diesel trio was not to be as impressive as that of PATRIOTIC, HEROIC and GRAPHIC. All three went to war, but only the ULSTER MONARCH returned to the Irish Sea. ULSTER QUEEN had the misfortune to run aground on the Isle of Man in February 1940, and was salvaged

with some difficulty. Whilst under repair she was requisitioned by the Admiralty and extensively converted to an anti-aircraft ship. Her war service was extensive, involving convoys to North Russia, Mediterranean landings and a voyage to the Far East to support planned landings in Malaya. On the return of peace the extent of the conversion was such that reconversion was uneconomic, and after four years in lay-up she was broken up in Belgium in 1950.

SOUTHERN RAVEN

Moore Shipbuilding Co., Oakland, California, USA; 1918, 6,664gt, 403 feet

One of the more unusual ships photographed by John MacRoberts was SOUTHERN RAVEN, in the Holy Loch in July 1950. One of many cargo steamers built in the USA at the end of the First World War, she was originally named

OSKAWA but probably saw little service until taken over by the Ministry of War Transport in April 1942. Her refrigerating machinery made her particularly useful, and seven of these turbine-driven ships came under British control, four being lost by U-boat attack. EMPIRE RAVEN was sold to Christian Salvesen in 1948 to be used as a refrigerated transport to support

the Leith company's South Atlantic whaling operations. She was intended to bring home whalemeat, but even rationed post-war Britain did not want to eat much of this meat, and SOUTHERN RAVEN was withdrawn after only four years. She arrived at Port Glasgow in November 1952 to be broken up by Smith and Houston Ltd.

INGE MAERSK (top)

Svendborg Skibs. & Mask., Svendborg; 1922, 1,489gt, 252 feet

The apparently simple 'Baltic' type steamer could come in a wide variety of styles, and INGE MAERSK displays an unusual, bridge-deck-extended-forwards configuration. The owner when the photograph was taken on 14th May 1930 was D/S Svendborg, part of the A.P. Möller empire: the modest Baltic trader making quite a contrast to the huge container ships this owner now operates. In 1938 INGE MAERSK was sold to Sweden and became TRIO, also carrying the names MERCIA and TIBRA in the next dozen years. In 1950 she helped the regeneration of the German merchant fleet, becoming the HARRIET SIEDLER. But at the end of the decade steamers were becoming obsolescent, and she was laid up at Lubeck in September 1958. It was almost two years later, however, that she was broken up at Wilhelmshafen.

TORNE (bottom)

Lindholmens Mek. Verks., Göteborg; 1912, 3,792gt, 359 feet

The ore carriers and later OBOs of Trafik A/B Grängesberg-Oxelösund were interesting visitors to the Mersey, perhaps giving the river its first taste of the classic ore carrier which later became so familiar. TORNE was a particularly early example, completed in 1912 for Rederi A/B Luleå-Ofoten, a company which merged to form Grängesberg-Oxelösund in 1916. TORNE had probably begun her voyage loading Swedish ore in the Norwegian port of Narvik, and it was here she met her end in April 1940. She was set on fire by British warships during the attempt to prevent the German invasion and scuttled two days later. This was not quite the end of her story, however, as she was refloated in June 1955 and her hulk towed to Stavanger for breaking up.

STAFFORDSHIRE

Fairfield Shipbuilding and Engineering Co. Ltd., Govan; 1929, 10,654gt, 484 feet

In the Mersey in April 1937, STAFFORDSHIRE looks a classic Bibby liner, with four tall masts and a profile almost unchanged since the first STAFFORDSHIRE had been built at Belfast in 1894. In spite of her tall funnel and anachronistic appearance, however, she was a motorship, one of three built in the late 1920s.

As for many passenger ships, the war had much in store for the ship. STAFFORDSHIRE was attacked by aircraft and almost sunk north west of Scotland in May 1941, but was reboarded by her crew and

beached. After repair on the Tyne she took part in landings in the south of France and went to Malaya at the war's end.

After a spell of peacetime trooping, which was familiar to most Bibby ships, she was extensively rebuilt in 1948-1949. She emerged with just one mast instead of four and a broader funnel: a profile which became as familiar for Bibby ships post-war as the four-master was pre-war. The company had another ten years' service from her on their Liverpool to Rangoon route. Sold her to Japanese breakers in 1959, her last voyage east was made as STAFFORD MARU.

DUBLIN GAS BOATS
Terry O'Conalláin

From the early years of the nineteenth century most Irish towns of any consequence had a gas supply. The gas manufactured in a local works was used for street and house lighting and later for domestic cooking. As Ireland is without any useful coal reserves it was necessary to import suitable coal from Britain. This gave employment to large fleets of sailing colliers, which began to be superseded by steam colliers in the latter part of the nineteenth century. The trade was to continue until natural gas made redundant both the manufacturing works and the attendant fleets of colliers.

In a large centre of population such as Dublin and its surrounding townships there was keen rivalry to supply the gas. The Alliance Gas Company was founded in 1835 while the Dublin Consumers Gas Company was established in 1844 and legally incorporated in 1845. Just two years later, in 1847, legislation allowed the formation of the Alliance & Dublin Consumers Gas Company. On 16th July 1866 certain restrictions in the 1847 Act were repealed and the Alliance & Dublin Consumers Gas Company amalgamated with the new Commercial Gas Company which had been registered on 4th February 1864.

There was still competition from the United General Gas Company which some years before had taken over the Hibernian Gas Company. However, this was not to last and the United General was soon absorbed by the Alliance & Dublin Consumers Gas Company. Thus, Dublin and its townships had one large company supplying its gas needs, watched keenly by the general population who were not slow to voice their criticisms, if one can believe the stories of vigorous letter-writing in the Dublin daily newspapers. One of these, *The Freeman's Journal*, was owned by Sir John Grey, a leading figure in the Gas Company.

Cross channel freight rates favoured the use of Dublin and the main gas works was conveniently situated adjacent to river berths and the docks of the Grand Canal Company at Ringsend. The tonnage figures for coal were reasonably constant at around one million tons per annum from 1874 onwards, when separate figures were first extracted. At that time 75% of this trade was carried by sailing collier. By the end of the century steam colliers dominated the trade and were gradually to take over completely.

Prominent in the coal trade were firms such as Tedcastle, McCormick & Company and Thos. Heiton & Company, but larger firms would also contract cargoes in their westbound ships. Many smaller local owners also relied on the trade as did others on the west coast of Britain where the principal coal exporting ports were located.

Facilities at Dublin

In Dublin the Gas Company had discharging facilities on Sir John Rogerson's Quay on the south side of the River Liffey. Using their own cranes they unloaded the coal into wagons on a light tramway system which ran around the corner into Forbes Street and thus into the gasworks.

The other berthage was alongside the works at the western end of Grand Canal Dock, where the gas company had cranes and overhead conveyors. Access to the dock from seawards was via the River Dodder and three locks of which only one – the easternmost – was suitable for sea-going vessels. It could only accommodate ships up to 150 feet in length making it a tight squeeze even for the Gas Company when it later acquired its own ships. Frequently, vessels leaving the dock had to enter the lock stern first and be warped to one side of the lock then the other so that the door-type gates could be closed. The Gas Company continued to use the river berths where there were no length restrictions so that the survival of its own fleet of colliers of less than 150 feet in length is surprising.

Colliers acquired

During the First World War the gasworks experienced difficulties in maintaining supplies and made the decision to acquire its own tonnage. On the Thames, the big London gas companies were making similar moves. The first ship was probably bought as a stop-gap to keep supplies coming in and was registered in the ownership of one of the Grey family rather than the Gas Company itself. The ARDRI (Gaelic for High King) was actually too big to use the lock into the Grand Canal Dock and had to discharge at the firm's non-appropriated berth on Sir John Rogerson's Quay.

The next ship purchased was the BRAEDALE in 1918. She came from the appropriately-named Thomas M. Collier, coal importer and merchant in the nearby port of Bray on the borders of Counties Dublin and Wicklow. BRAEDALE was registered in the ownership of the Alliance & Dublin Consumers Gas Company. Her dimensions meant she could use the Camden Lock into Ringsend.

The ARDRI and BRAEDALE were evidently considered a success, as two new ships were ordered from Lytham in Lancashire. There is evidence from contemporary *Lloyd's Registers* that the first was intended to be named ALLIANCE, but she was completed in May 1920 as GLENAGEARY (Gaelic GLEANN NA GCAORACH - valley or glen of the sheep) and registered at Dublin with signal hoist KGPC. In October 1921 the GLENCULLEN (Gaelic

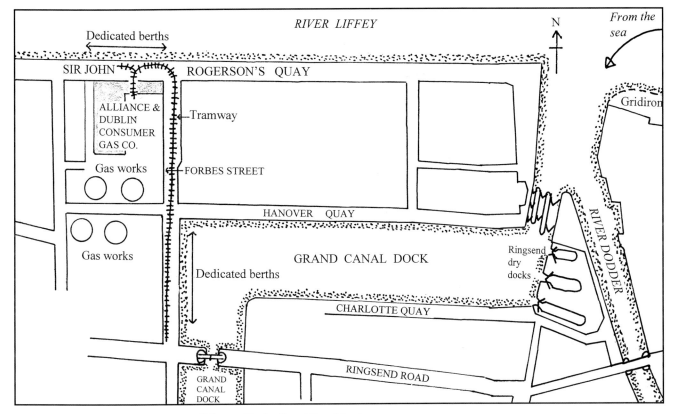

The Gas Company's berths on the River Liffey and in the Grand Canal Dock.

GLEANN CHUILLIN - holly glen) entered service. Measuring just seven inches longer than her sister ship at 142.7 feet she was designed to use the Camden Lock from the River Dodder into Grand Canal Dock. No signal hoist is recorded for her until the early thirties when she was allocated EIKD and GLENAGEARY was changed to EIDV. With the GLENAGEARY and GLENCULLEN in service, BRAEDALE and ARDRI were sold.

Trading patterns

Both ships soon settled down into the Irish Sea collier trade. Carrying around 440 tons of cargo each ship had a crew of 11 consisting of master, mate, two engineers, three deckhands, three firemen and a cook. With a steaming time of 14 hours from the Mersey to the Liffey and allowing for locking in and out on either side, three round trips could be achieved each

GLENCULLEN alongside the Gas Company's berth in the Grand Canal Dock.

GLENAGEARY loading coal in Bramley-Moore Dock, Liverpool (top). The high level coal railway was built between 1880 and 1882 to link the Lancashire coalfield directly with Liverpool Docks in an attempt to improve coal handling at the port. The hydraulic crane about to lift a wagon is part of the original equipment, supplied by Armstrongs of Newcastle.

GLENAGEARY and GLENCREE wait to lock in from the River Dodder on 19th May 1963 (middle). When the tide fell, GLENCREE was in the channel and stayed upright, but GLENAGEARY was caught on the edge of the channel and leant rather drunkenly on her fleet mate. [Author]

The launch of GLENCREE at Dublin. Note the pale band at the waterline (bottom).

week in good weather. In winter, however, the ships would often dodge for shelter in Moelfre Bay on the North Wales coast or behind the Isle of Man and this, especially when combined with fog at the mouth of the Mersey, could knock the ships back to one trip a week.

On various occasions the ships were seen on outside work, particularly in summertime when there was less demand for gas. In August 1926, for instance, the GLENAGEARY loaded gravel at Arklow for Birkenhead. In 1932 the economic war between the UK and the Irish Free State reached its height and the GLENCULLEN became the only one of the Gas Company's steamers to make continental passages when she loaded three cargoes of coal at Rotterdam for Dublin.

Well pleased with their own ships, the Gas Company decided to reduce their chartering requirements by building a third ship of similar dimensions. The order this time went to Dublin Dockyard and the GLENCREE (Gaelic GLEANN CRIOTHAIGH –

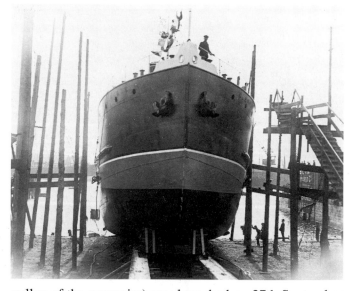

valley of the quagmire) was launched on 27th September 1934 and ran trials in early November. Her gross tonnage was higher than the earlier ships, at 481 tons.

Locking in and out

The method of locking in and out at Ringsend was interesting and even at the end of the steamer era the author has seen up to six ships jostling for position. To lock in ships entered the chamber from the River Dodder. Turning hard to starboard past the Ringsend Dockyard – which dry-docked them – ships such as Heiton's motor vessel SAINT EUNAN (437/1936) and Wallace Brothers' RINGWALL (407/1921) or BROSWALL (312/1921) as well as the gas boats and others proceeded to their respective berths in the inner and outer docks.

Locking out often saw many of the largest ships such as the GLENs enter the chamber stern first. This enabled the sharper bow to be winched to one side or other of the Camden Lock to permit the door-type gates to be closed in turn.

Gas boats at war

This orderly state of affairs continued until 1939. On 28th September 1939 Mr FJ Dickens addressed a meeting of the Alliance and Dublin Consumers Gas Company as follows:

'All precautions that would have been taken have in fact been taken and coal stocks accumulated to the limit of our storage capacity'.

A strike of coal trimmers lost four weeks of imports but matters were not unsatisfactory until 1941 when there were severe restrictions on coal imports from the UK. Prudent as always, and remembering their experience in the First World War, the Gas Company had taken steps to acquire a fourth ship which, however, had to remain registered in Britain for the duration. Renamed GLENBRIDE (Gaelic GLEANN BHRIDE - (St) Bride's Glen) she was under various nominal ownerships until 1949 when brought into company ownership with the call sign EIQL. Like the other ships she was named after a beauty spot in the hills south of Dublin.

The Second World War saw the fleet painted in neutral colours except for the GLENBRIDE which, according to anecdotal evidence, continued in peace-time colours and was unarmed. A number of ships owned in the Free State were registered in Britain but manned and operated locally. For example, Heiton's SAINT EUNAN was registered in Troon and armed but, again according to anecdotal evidence, traded in Heiton's colours. These UK-registered ships continued in their usual trades and thus were in a unique position, Irish owned and manned, technically at war, but engaged in 'normal' trades to and from their neutral bases.

The conflict was to see the GLENs attacked despite their neutrality markings, although curiously the GLENBRIDE seems to have led a charmed existence. In fact, the ships were free from harassment until 21st March 1941 when both the GLENCULLEN and GLENCREE were attacked by aircraft. Sailing in company from Barry towards Dublin the GLENCULLEN (Captain Waldron) was attacked at 5.20 pm some seven miles west of Helvick Light Vessel. A plane flew from directly astern and machine-gunned the ship despite her clearly visible neutrality markings. Slight damage was caused and later at 7.00 pm there was another attack involving the dropping of a bomb which fell

Entering Grand Canal Docks via Camden Lock from the River Dodder is GLENBRIDE. This is a post-war view: she is registered in Dublin. [World Ship Photo Library]

astern. GLENCREE was also attacked at 5.20 pm seven miles west of Helvick Light Vessel: a bomb was dropped and fell about 40 feet off the starboard side. There was some damage to the dynamo and bilge pumps. Again at 7.00 pm GLENCREE was machine gunned but both vessels proceeded and docked at Dublin the next day.

On the following day the SAINT FINTAN (495/1921) of Dublin was bombed and lost with all nine hands whilst on passage from Drogheda to Cardiff. On 26th March 1941 the Dungarvan-owned THE LADY BELLE (341/1900) under Captain Thomas Donohue was bombed: the missile penetrated the forecastle head and passed out through the ship's side. The motor ship EDENVALE (444/1936) was also attacked so that Taoiseach Mr. Eamon de Valera addressed the Dail about these attacks on unarmed colliers. *Inter alia* he said:

> 'In all cases the attacking aircraft was identified as German. The Chargé d'Affaires in Berlin has been instructed to protest and claim compensation for the damage done.'

The GLENAGEARY under Captain Simpson was attacked ten miles north of South Bishop Lighthouse on 17th May 1941. Three bombs were dropped after which the aircraft returned to machine gun the ship. No injuries were sustained and the vessel continued safely on the voyage from Newport to Dublin. Later that same year, on 25th October, she was on passage from Barry to Dublin under Captain Edward Kelly when a German plane dropped two bombs which missed when she was some ten miles south-east of the South Arklow Buoy. The aircraft then attacked the ship with machine gun fire five times before departing. However, there were no injuries and GLENAGEARY completed her passage to Dublin.

In a re-run of the first incident the GLENCULLEN and GLENCREE were attacked in November 1941. GLENCULLEN under Captain Jones left Barry for Dublin on 4th November, broke away from the convoy off Milford and proceeded towards Dublin in company with GLENCREE, John Kelly's steamer PORTAVOGIE (869/1934) and two Dutch motorships. At 6.30 pm on 5th November she was attacked by a German aircraft despite her clear markings and subjected to two machine-gun attacks. The PORTAVOGIE opened fire on the plane and drove it off. The GLENCREE (Captain CH Bodels) was also machine-gunned and the Chief Engineer WB Brown and the Second Engineer M Moore were both wounded. The ship altered course for Fishguard where the latter was landed and taken to hospital. GLENCULLEN had no casualties and proceeded. She returned a favour to PORTAVOGIE by escorting her to Dublin Bay as the Kelly ship's compass was out of order. They parted company at the Kish Light Vessel.

There were no further attacks on the ships. GLENBRIDE, registered in Glasgow, is not recorded as experiencing any attacks: such are the fortunes of war as they affected civilian merchant seafarers as they went about their daily tasks.

Throughout the war the Gas Company continued purchasing oil as feedstock for gasification. Even in the worst days of the war this continued to arrive regularly from Curacao. Coal sometimes came across the Irish Sea in unusual vessels, including ocean-going ships such as IRISH BEECH (2,002/1884).

The ending of the war did not end the dramas which the steamers experienced. In August 1945 the GLENCULLEN, on passage from Belfast to Maryport, ran aground on the Mull of Galloway. After refloating she was beached at Drummore at noon on 12th August. She had been holed amidships and was taken to Stranraer for temporary repairs.

Motor colliers

As steamers gradually gave way to motorships on the Irish Sea the gas boats became an anachronism although – always well kept – they looked stately compared with diminutive motorships lying at other berths in the canal dock. These included such regulars as William Robertson's PRASE (374/1938) and CAIRNGORM (394/1938), ICI's POLYTHENE

Photography was not permitted in Dublin during the Second World War, but an apprentice at the Ringsend Dockyard took this shot of GLENAGEARY as she dropped down to the locks during March 1942 (left). Despite the very apparent neutrality markings, GLENAGEARY was attacked several times by German aircraft in the Irish Sea. [Author's collection, courtesy the late J. Butler]

After renaming GLENBRIDE, the motor coaster LADY SYLVIA lost both her mainmast and the white paint on her deckhouses in favour of the drab brown which was traditional for colliers. She is seen here in Liverpool Docks (opposite page). [World Ship Photo Library]

(330/1949), the motorships of the Ramsey Shipping Company, and the 400-ton Dutchmen in from Antwerp with silver sand for the glass bottle works on Ringsend Road. The Gas Company themselves chartered vessels capable of using Ringsend Dock, including the Dutch ships NOORDERHAVEN (376/1951) and CITADEL (369/1950).

By the early 1960s the steamers – probably looking better than ever – were becoming costly to operate and the efficient little motorships highlighted this. During 1963 and 1964 they were all sold for scrap and in their place just two motorships were acquired which took the traditional names GLENBRIDE and GLENCULLEN.

The LADY SYLVIA first arrived at Grand Canal Dock in the spring of 1963 and berthed outside the GLENCREE and ahead of GLENCULLEN where the contrast between the brown and black of the steamers and the bright blue and white of the motorship was very evident. By May 1963 she had a black hull with the Gas Company funnel and white superstructure and bulwarks on the forecastle. Still bearing the name LADY SYLVIA she was now registered in Dublin. During the summer months her derricks and masts were removed and brown was applied to the after housing. She looked decidedly dowdy compared with her previous Rochester owners' bright livery. Later that summer she was renamed GLENBRIDE.

In November 1963 the GLENCREE went off to the Netherlands for scrapping which was rather appropriate as the Dutch coaster WALCHEREN was

the second motorship bought. 5th January 1964 saw the new ship on the blocks in Dublin dry-dock. Her new name had already been cut into her hull, but in the event she started trading as the WALCHEREN of Dublin without any change in livery but flying a huge Irish tricolour as she locked out of Ringsend Dock. Very shortly afterwards she was renamed GLENCULLEN and given a black hull. She lost her derricks for a while and, inevitably, her deck housing was painted dark brown but this was later modified by adding small areas of white, first to deck edgings and later to all the housing.

For the next few years the motor colliers imported coal for the Gas Company but for their last 18 months or so were out tramping. GLENCULLEN was given her derricks back and ran regularly from the Bristol Channel to Limerick and Ballylongford, a hard passage into the teeth of the Atlantic on her wintertime voyages. Among other places visited were the Cornish ports, near-Continental ports and Drogheda, Dundalk, Belfast, and Portrush. One unusual cargo was slate to Jersey from Palnackie where she was said to be the first commercial caller for 21 years. But the two fleet sisters now seldom saw each other, and the end was definitely in sight. In 1968 GLENCULLEN went to her fleet sister's former owners, Thomas Watson, as LADY SABINA and in 1969 GLENBRIDE was sold to Alderney owners.

By 1968 the Gas Company had completely changed over to oil, achieving an annual saving of £266,000, but even this traffic was to end following the discovery of a natural gas field 27 miles south of the Old Head of Kinsale in September 1971.

Fleet list

1. ARDRI   1916-1923   Steel and iron

O.N. 99819   477g   192n   165.2 x 26.1 x 10.8 feet
C. 2-cyl. by Ross and Duncan, Govan.
28.5.1892: Launched by J. Shearer and Son, Kelvinhaugh, Glasgow (Yard No.8).
11.6.1892: Registered in the ownership of William Robertson, Glasgow as CORAL.
6.2.1915: Sold to James McKelvie (James Steele Smith, trading as Eirinn Steamers Co., managers), Edinburgh.
24.5.1915: Renamed ARDRI.
20.7.1916: Acquired by William J. Grey, Dublin (James Steele Smith, Edinburgh, manager).
29.5.1917: William J. Grey became manager.
11.10.1923: Sold to John and William Thomas, trading as William Thomas and Sons, Amlwch.
22.1.1936: Sprang a leak and sank thirteen miles west of Bardsey whilst on a voyage from London to Glasgow with a cargo of cement.
7.2.1936: Register closed.

2. BRAEDALE   1918-1920

O.N.104581   405g   161n   142.2 x 25.0 x 11.1 feet
T. 3-cyl. by Muir & Houston, Glasgow.
10.1894: Completed by Murdoch & Murray, Port Glasgow (Yard No.125).
29.10.1894: Registered in the ownership of John B. Barr, Glasgow as BESSIE BARR.
7.10.1895: Sold to Robert B. Ballantyne and Co., Glasgow.
6.1.1914: Sold to Thomas M. Collier, Wicklow.
4.6.1915: Renamed BRAEDALE.
10.1.1918: Acquired by the Alliance & Dublin Consumer Gas Company (William J. Grey, manager), Dublin.
9.3.1920: Sold to David Hudson, Middlesbrough and Ernest Varley, Redcar.
4.4.1922: Sold to Samuel Thubron, South Shields.
20.3.1929: Sold to the Eltham Shipping Co. Ltd. (George Canning, manager), Wallasey.
18.7.1931: Sold to John Gillespie, Liverpool.
16.10.1932: Foundered about eight miles south west of the Needles whilst on a voyage from Dieppe to Bristol with a cargo of apples.
9.1.1933: Register closed.

Bought to serve the Dublin gas works, ARDRI, was registered in the ownership of company secretary William J. Grey. She is at Eastham in the colours of William Thomas of Amlwch, to whom she was sold in 1923 (above).

The letter T on BRAEDALE's funnel suggests that this photograph was taken between 1922 and 1929 when owned by Samuel Thubron of South Shields (left). *[Author's collection]*

GLENAGEARY makes her only transit of the Caledonian Canal with a coal cargo from the north east of England which was used for purifying purposes (opposite page top). GLENAGEARY and GLENCULLEN (opposite bottom) bore a strong family resemblance to coasters from the same Lytham yard for Liverpool's Zillah Shipping and Carrying Co. Ltd., which began with ASHFIELD (436/1914).

3. ALLIANCE/GLENAGEARY 1920-1964
O.N.140469   464g 182n 142.0 x 25.8 x 11.5 feet
T. 3-cyl. by Lytham Shipbuilding & Engineering Co. Ltd., Lytham.
21.2.1920: Launched by the Lytham Shipbuilding & Engineering Co. Ltd., Lytham (Yard No.578). It was originally intended to name her ALLIANCE, and she was launched as such.
5.1920: Completed for the Alliance & Dublin Consumer Gas Company, Dublin as GLENAGEARY.
1.12.1964: Demolition commenced by the Hammond Lane Metal Co. Ltd., Dublin.

4. GLENCULLEN (1)   1921-1963
O.N.144974 466g 177n 142.7 x 26.0 x 11.5 feet
T. 3-cyl. by Lytham Shipbuilding & Engineering Co. Ltd., Lytham.
5.8.1921: Launched by the Lytham Shipbuilding & Engineering Co. Ltd., Lytham (Yard No.600).
10.1921: Completed for the Alliance & Dublin Consumer Gas Company, Dublin as GLENCULLEN.
5.1963: Sold to Lithgows Ltd. who stripped her at their Kingston Yard at Greenock.
6.1963: Filled with stone and cement and sunk as a breakwater at the estate of Sir William Lithgow.

5. GLENCREE   1934-1963

O.N.159301   481g   187n   142.0 x 26.0 x 11.5 feet
T. 3-cyl. by Aitchison, Blair Ltd., Clydebank.
27.9.1934: Launched by the Dublin Dockyard Co. (Vickers, Ireland) Ltd., Dublin (Yard No.159).
12.1934: Completed for the Alliance & Dublin Consumer Gas Company, Dublin as GLENCREE.
8.11.1963: Delivered to N.V. De Koophandel for breaking up at Nieuw Lekkerland, Holland.

6. GLENBRIDE (1)   1949-1963

O.N.143608   440g   168n   143.2 x 25.1 x 12.0 feet
C.2-cyl. by Ailsa Shipbuilding Co. Ltd., Troon.
4.12.1919: Launched by the Ailsa Shipbuilding Co. Ltd., Troon (Yard No.372).
29.12.1919: Completed for the Summerfield Steamship Co. Ltd., Liverpool as JESSIE SUMMERFIELD.
14.3.1927: Sold to the Zillah Shipping and Carrying Co. Ltd. (W.A. Savage, manager), Liverpool.
19.3.1927: Sold to William Robertson Ltd., Glasgow.
21.4.1927: Renamed MORION.
21.11.1939: Sold to the Mohochang Exploration Co. Ltd. (J. Galbraith of Stephenson, Clarke & Associated Companies, manager), Manchester.
8.12.1939: Renamed GLENBRIDE.

27.5.1942: Sold to Chatterley Whitfield Collieries Ltd. (J. Galbraith, manager), Stoke-on-Trent.
18.2.1946: Sold to the Polgarth Steamship Co. Ltd. (James Macmillan, manager), London.
20.10.1949: Owner became the Alliance & Dublin Consumer Gas Company, Dublin
10.4.1963: Haulbowline Industries Ltd. commenced demolition at Passage West, Cork.

7. GLENBRIDE (2)   1963-1969

O.N.400370   371g   175n   147.3 x 25.1 x 9.8 feet
Oil engines 2SCSA 6-cylinder by Crossley Brothers Ltd., Manchester.
19.1.1952: Launched by Philip & Son Ltd., Dartmouth (Yard No. 1234) for Thomas Watson (Shipping) Ltd., Rochester as LADY SYLVIA.
4.1952: Completed.
1963: Acquired by the Alliance & Dublin Consumer Gas Company, Dublin and renamed GLENBRIDE.
1969: Sold to the Alderney Shipping Co. Ltd., Alderney and renamed ALDERNEY TRADER.
1973: Sold to the Gemini Shipping Co. Ltd., Famagusta, Cyprus and renamed MEMI.
13.12.1977: Seized at Cherbourg and sold to T.I.M.A.C., St.Malo, France for conversion to a pontoon.

GLENCREE leaves the Mersey in 1956, well laden with coal, and burning copious quantities (above). Rather a stubby little craft, the only gas boat built in Ireland did not have the elegance of Lytham-built steamers. Note that she has lost the white or yellow waterline with which she and some of the other colliers were built.

GLENBRIDE, also in the Mersey (left). The slight list probably indicates full bunkers: as the coal from the port bunkers was burnt she would gradually come upright, as she is when arriving at Dublin on page 149.

8. GLENCULLEN (2)   1963-1968

O.N.335991   440g 221n 149.3 x 23.9 x 10.9 feet
Oil engines 4SCSA 8-cylinder by Maschinenbau Kiel
A.G., Kiel, West Germany.
18.10.1952: Launched by Scheepsbouw. A. Apol, Wirdum,
Holland (Yard No.169) for W. Smid (N.V.
Scheepsvaartkantoor 'Groningen' managers), Groningen,
Holland as WALCHEREN.
1952: Completed.
1963: Acquired by the Alliance & Dublin Consumer Gas

Company, Dublin and renamed GLENCULLEN.
1968: Sold to Thomas Watson (Shipping) Ltd., Rochester
and renamed LADY SABINA.
1973: Sold to Thames Services (Marine) Ltd., Tilbury and
renamed TREMONT.
1975: Sold to unknown owners and renamed HUZEIFA.
1976: Sold to Hamza Maritime Freight Agency, Dubai and
renamed MUMTAZ.
6.1998: Deleted from *Lloyd's Register*, continued
existence in doubt.

Photographed on 4th May 1963, soon after arriving for the first time at Dublin, the LADY SYLVIA was still registered in Rochester but had the Gas Company's black funnel with a white letter G already been painted up (left). She was registered in Dublin on 20th May, but still as LADY SYLVIA: renaming as GLENBRIDE had to wait until later that summer. [Author]

When bought, both the motor colliers had derricks, but these were removed as unnecessary for the coal trade, where both loading and unloading was by shoreside equipment. However, when the Dublin coal trade declined and the motorships were more and more sent tramping, derrricks were replaced. GLENCULLEN (2) has her derricks at Sir John Rogerson's Quay (below).

WHALE SHIP CONVERSIONS
Part Three
Peter Newall

ROYAL MAIL CONVERSIONS

A number of ships belonging to the Royal Mail group ended their careers as whalers. Among the most famous conversions were the SALVESTRIA and SOURABAYA which were owned by Christian Salvesen of Leith.

SOURABAYA
Workman, Clark and Co. Ltd., Belfast; 1915, 10,107gt, 470 feet
Just before the First World War, Royal Mail ordered a group of large cargo ships for their newly acquired Shire Line – the first

two, CARDIGANSHIRE and CARNARVON-SHIRE (this page, top), twin screwed, with gross tonnages of 9,400, were followed by a 7,800gt, single-screw pair CARMARTHEN-SHIRE and PEMBROKESHIRE.

The quartet survived the war, and in 1929 CARDIGANSHIRE and her smaller running mate CARMARTHENSHIRE were sold to Salvesens who sent them to Smith's Dock River Tees Dockyard, South Bank for conversion into the whale factory ships SALVESTRIA and SOURABAYA – the latter

is shown (opposite and bottom at Brixham) shortly after completion. Despite their size difference, they had very similar profiles and were difficult to tell apart. Sadly both were lost during the war. The SALVESTRIA was first to go in 1940 when she hit an acoustic mine in the Firth of Forth, whilst SOURABAYA was torpedoed in 1942 during a voyage from New York to the Clyde. *[Opposite: Salvesen Collection, University of Edinburgh; top: A. Duncan; bottom: Lawrence Dunn]*

HIGHLANDERS

To transport prime beef from their flourishing family meat business near Buenos Aires, the brothers Hugh and William Nelson bought the 3,000gt SPINDRIFT in 1889 and renamed her HIGHLAND SCOT. This was the start of the famous Nelson Line which was acquired by Royal Mail in 1913.

THORLAND

Russell and Co., Port Glasgow; 1903, 5,201gt, 385 feet

In 1901 Nelson Line started carrying passengers, and during the next three years six new ships were built, all with large cold storage facilities and accommodation for a limited number of first class passengers. HIGHLAND ENTERPRISE (top) was one of these, and remained with the company until 1929 when she was bought by J. Bennett (Billingsgate) Ltd. of London, and converted into a mother ship for trawlers fishing off Greenland. The next year she was sold again and transformed into the fish factory ship NORTHLAND. Her final name THORLAND was given by the London Whaling Co. when she became a whale ship in 1932. She is seen in the second photograph, arriving at Great Yarmouth in October 1934 to refrigerate herrings. Seized by the Germans at Sandefjord in 1940, THORLAND spent the rest of the war as a storage ship. Owned by various companies after 1946, she was sold for scrap in 1951. *[Upper: A. Duncan; lower: Kevin O' Donoghue collection]*

CALPEAN STAR

Harland & Wolff Ltd., Belfast; 1929, 14,131gt, 523 feet

Between 1928 and 1930 Harland & Wolff built a new class of five, twin-funnelled, motor-driven passenger liners for Nelson Line. HIGHLAND CHIEFTAIN was the second in the series. With passenger accommodation in the 'Old English' style, they also had over 500,000 cubic feet of cargo space, mostly insulated. Having survived the war virtually unscathed, HIGHLAND CHIEFTAIN returned to the River Plate service in 1948, and was the first of the group to be sold in 1959.

She was bought by the Calpe Shipping Co. of Gibraltar, which was established in 1956 by Alfredo Ryan, a British subject, born in Gibraltar and who settled in Argentina in 1924. Ryan became a key player in the whaling industry in 1944, when he took control of the first ever Antarctic whaling company, the Compañia Argentina de Pesca. With the support of President Peron, in 1947 Ryan contracted Harland & Wolff to build the world's largest whale factory ship, the 24,570gt JUAN PERON, but financial scandal and delays meant that Ryan was unable to pay for the ship and it was seized by the Argentine government and turned into a tanker. HIGHLAND CHIEFTAIN was bought for use as a frozen meat transporter to and from South Georgia, but in 1960 her new career as CALPEAN STAR came to an abrupt end when she partially sank off Montevideo after her engine room flooded - her remains were visible for a number of years. *[Both: Peter Newall collection]*

NORTH ATLANTIC LINERS

SOLGLIMT was one of the whalers that had been a North Atlantic liner. She was unique not only as the first passenger liner owned by Svenska-Amerika Linien, but also as a ship which had four different funnels.

SOLGLIMT
Blohm und Voss, Hamburg, Germany; 1900, 12,606gt, 571 feet

Around the turn of the century the Nederlandsch-Amerikaansche Stoomvaart Mij. (Holland-America Line) introduced

three new sisters on to their Rotterdam to New York service. These were POTSDAM, RIJNDAM and NOORDAM and, instead of giving the order to their traditional builders Harland & Wolff, the company turned to Blohm und Voss for the first in the trio, POTSDAM. From the outset, the German-built ship, although similar to her Harland sisters, suffered from major problems. On her first voyage her awning deck broke up in rough weather and had to be replaced and, a year later, she had her funnel lengthened by some 23 feet to improve her furnaces' draught, making the stack one of the largest on the Atlantic run. In 1915 she was bought by the Rederei Sverige-

Nordamerika Linien (known as Svenska-Amerika Linien from 1925) of Göteborg as their first passenger liner STOCKHOLM (upper). A neutral during the war, she was converted to oil firing in 1922 and her funnel was shortened. Around the same time, she had her first running mate, DROTTNINGHOLM, formerly Allan Line's VIRGINIAN.

With the arrival in 1928 of GRIPSHOLM, the first large North Atlantic motorship, STOCKHOLM was no longer required and she was sold to Hvalfangerselk. Atlas A/S (Chr. Nielsen & Co.) of Larvik for conversion to a whale factory ship. Completely altered at the Götaverken shipyard, Göteborg, her superstructure reduced considerably, with a new upright funnel, she was named SOLGLIMT. In 1931, she joined the Thor Dahl fleet and ten years later was captured by the German raider PINGUIN along with OLE WEGGER and PELAGOS. Taken to Bordeaux, she became the German tanker SONDERBURG and was scuttled in Cherbourg in 1944 – her remains were refloated in 1947 and towed away for scrap.

The lower photograph shows OLE WEGGER (left), SOLGLIMT (middle) and THORSHAMMER (right) during their summer lay-up at Sandefjord. *[Upper: Peabody Museum, Salem; lower: Ambrose Greenway collection]*

PHOENIX ARISEN

Another product of Blohm und Voss was HAMBURG which, unlike SOLGLIMT, was raised after the war and was given another career as the Russian YURI DOLGORUKI.

YURI DOLGORUKI

Blohm und Voss, Hamburg, Germany; 1926, 21,132gt, 635 feet

One of the quartet of liners known as the Ballin-class, which were built for Hamburg-Amerika Line in the mid 1920s, HAMBURG (top) and her sisters were very popular liners on the Atlantic. Much of their appeal was due to the fact that they were designed to be the exact opposite of the grand statements of national pride which personified German liners before the war. Turbine driven, they were fitted with anti-rolling tanks and their comfortable, unpretentious accommodation attracted many American and British passengers. The last two built, HAMBURG and NEW YORK, differed from ALBERT BALLIN and DEUTSCHLAND in having two masts instead of four, although all four underwent considerable change throughout their careers with HAPAG.

Used for most of the war as an accommodation ship for the German Navy at Gdynia, in 1945 HAMBURG took part in the mass evacuation of Germans from the occupied Eastern territories. During one of these voyages she struck two mines and sank at Sassnitz. She was raised in 1950 by the Russians who decided to have her refitted again as a passenger liner, becoming YURI DOLGORUKI. After ten years she was nearly complete when plans were changed and she became a whale factory ship (middle). In her fiftieth year she was withdrawn from service and scrapped in 1977. *[Peter Newall collection]*

AN OLD ROLLER

READY

Barclay, Curle & Co. Ltd., Glasgow; 1897, 4,324gt, 384 feet

Designed for Castle Line's intermediate service to South Africa, RAGLAN CASTLE and her sister DUNOLLY CASTLE proved to be too small and tended to roll badly in poor weather. When only seven years old RAGLAN CASTLE was acquired by her builders Barclay, Curle who resold her, apparently to the Russian Government as a naval store ship during the Russo-Japanese War, when she was renamed HANNA. Soon afterwards, with the Russians defeated, she was bought by the Danish East Asiatic Co. as ST. DOMINGO. Returned again to her builders in 1908, she reverted to RAGLAN CASTLE and was used as a tramp on the North Atlantic for a year until her purchase by Donaldson Line who named her PYTHIA. Her whaling career commenced in 1911 when sold to the Dominion Whaling Co. of Sandefjord. With an unaltered name, she came under Thor Dahl control in the 1920s, and in 1929 capsized whilst undergoing repairs at Sandefjord. Raised, she was sold as READY, and was eventually broken up at Rosyth in 1934. *[Lawrence Dunn collection]*

ANOTHER DONALDSON

BRANSFIELD

Short Brothers Ltd., Sunderland; 1920, 6,865gt, 419 feet

In 1923 Donaldson Line formed the Donaldson South America Line to transport frozen meat from the River Plate to Europe and North American ports. Five refrigerated ships were specially built for this operation, all with Spanish names beginning with the letter C and, like most Donaldson cargo ships up to the 1930s, with counter sterns. CORDILLERA was one of these ships and, presumably because of her cold storage facilities, she was bought in 1948 by the Hector Whaling Co. of London who used her as the store ship BRANSFIELD until she went to the breakers in 1958. *[Lawrence Dunn collection]*

CABLE SHIPS

THULE

Blohm und Voss, Hamburg, Germany; 1926, 7,481gt, 434 feet

Intrigued as a teenager as to why THULE had a reduced clipper bow, it was only years later that I discovered she had previously been a cable ship. Built in the same year as the HAMBURG, NEPTUN (a popular German cable ship name) was a dual-purpose vessel and could operate either as an oil tanker or cable ship. As new, she laid a German-owned cable to the US which meant that Germany no longer had to rely on foreign communication networks. After the war, she was taken as reparations by the British Government, who sold her to Hector Whaling as the supply ship and whale oil transporter THULE. Soon after the sale of Hector's whaling fleet to Japan, she went for scrap to Belgium in 1961.
[Peter Newall]

THORODD

Wigham Richardson & Co., Newcastle-upon-Tyne; 1902, 7,981 gt, 487 feet

When built, COLONIA was the largest cable ship in the world and was ordered by the Telegraph and Maintenance Co. in order to lay the Pacific Cable Board's cable from Vancouver to Australia and New Zealand. After laying 80,700 nautical miles of cable, she was sold in 1928 to Thor Dahl and converted into the factory ship THORODD. After two seasons, she was laid up and sold in 1934 for further use as the whaler SYDIS. Just before the war, she was bought by a German firm and renamed SÜDMEER. As a depot ship, she was torpedoed and sunk by Russian aircraft in October 1944, near Honningsvaag, Norway.
[A. Duncan]

DUTCH THREAT

WILLEM BARENDSZ

A/B Götaverken, Göteborg, Sweden; 1931, 15,500gt, 504 feet

Despite their involvement in the manufacture of margarine, the Dutch did not get seriously into the whaling business until after the war when, in 1946, the Nederlandsche Maatschappij Voor De Walvischvaart N.V. (Vinke and Co.) of Amsterdam bought the motor tanker PAN GOTHIA and converted her into the factory ship WILLEM BARENDSZ.

Named after the 16th century Dutch arctic explorer, the WILLEM BARENDSZ was an unusual looking ship with four funnels. Renamed BLOEMENDAEL in 1955 (opposite page), the company gave her name to a new WILLEM BARENDSZ which was the largest whaling ship yet built. In 1961 she was sold to Japanese owners who converted her back to a tanker, the NITTO MARU. Sold again in 1964 as the NICHIEI MARU, she went for scrap in 1966. *[Fotoflite incorporating Skyfotos]*

The WILLEM BARENDSZ was also fitted with a Walrus flying boat, which meant there was now no escape for the whales. *[Opposite page bottom: Lawrence Dunn collection]*

ANTIQUES IN THE HUMBER

The work of photographers such as Marcus Barnard, who was active at Hull from 1900 onwards, have left us not only with an invaluable record of contemporary activity in their local ports, but also with images of ships belonging to previous generations. This feature presents a selection of steamers from the latter half of the nineteenth century, chosen for their actual – or their look of – antiquity.

Marcus Barnard, who was deaf and dumb, formed a number of partnerships. From about 1901 he traded as Gladstone and Barnard, and by 1903 he was advertising himself as a picture postcard dealer in partnership with a Mr. Stevenson. Probably his best known partnership was that with Thomas Straker, who was on the staff of the Hull Daily Mail. Barnard is known to have traded up until at least 1927.

MILAN (above)
John Reid and Co., Port Glasgow; 1855, 1,359gt, 286 feet
The ship in this photo looked like it had a tale to tell, and so it proved. The iron steamer MILAN was built for John Bibby, Son and Co. of Liverpool in the early days of their Liverpool and Mediterranean Screw Steam Shipping Company. The raking stem suggests she originally had a clipper bow, probably prior to 1877 when she was lengthened and had her two-cylinder engine compounded. Illustrations of her contemporaries in the Bibby fleet – of which there were many – show them carrying a full suit of sails. It seems possible the two masts remaining, although cut down somewhat, may have survived from this period: certainly they are quite inadequate for cargo handling, and derricks are singularly lacking.

Bibby sold MILAN in 1871 and she joined the Hull-based fleet of Wm. Brown, Atkinson and Co. who retained her name: this being a time when Board of Trade regulations meant ships were not renamed lightly. Brown, Atkinson's black funnel with white band was applied to both the funnel and its accompanying stove pipe:

under Bibby ownership she is said to have had two funnels placed abreast. Brown, Atkinson traded to the Baltic, as is evident from MILAN's timber deck cargo, which gives her the almost inevitable list.

Wm. Brown, Atkinson and Co. certainly got their money's worth out of MILAN, which traded for them for 36 years, until an accident at Hull finished her career. On 18th September 1907 she struck the lock head in Alexandra Dock whilst leaving for Rotterdam, and sank in the middle of the dock, with eight feet of water over her deck. Over a week went by before the WRECKER of the East Coast Salvage Company arrived to begin work on MILAN, and she was raised on 7th October. After drydocking the 52-year old hull was sold to France, presumably for breaking up.

NAUTILUS (opposite page top)
Bergsunds M.V., Stockholm, Sweden; 1872, 974gt, 209 feet
Sails were fitted to most early steamers, but photographs of them actually set are quite rare, as by the time the ship reached river or harbour the sails would usually have been stowed. This makes Barnard's shot of the Swedish steamer NAUTILUS particularly

notable, as do the boatmen at work.

This was another iron steamer with a very long life, spent essentially under one company's ownership, although its name changed several times. NAUTILUS was built for Stockholms Ångfartygs Rederibolag, which on becoming a limited company in 1895 changed its name subtly so that its last element become Rederiaktiebolag. This title being a little cumbersome, the company was generally known as Sankt-Eriksbolaget, or the St. Eric company, after its flag which carried the crowned head of St. Erik, the patron saint of Stockholm. In December 1907 all the company's ships passed to Nya Rederiaktiebolaget Svea, being paid for by a new issue of shares in Svea. However, the shareholders in the Stockholm company wanted some lasting remembrance of their old company, and in 1908 the owners were renamed Stockholms Rederiaktiebolaget Svea. This title sufficed for the remaining career of NAUTILUS, which was broken up by Lindholmens Varv at Gothenburg in 1935. Sixty-two years is an impressive life for a ship, but this period under only one owner is exceptional.

MUNCASTER (above)
Whitehaven Shipbuilding Co., Whitehaven;
1874, 889gt, 233 feet
MUNCASTER was also Swedish, owned by
Ångfartygs Aktieb. Esperance of
Helsingborg. However, her origins go back
to the beginnings of a well-known British
company, Coast Lines, one of whose
constituents was the fleet of John Bacon
of Liverpool. Bacon had MUNCASTER built

and used her in his coastal and deep sea
sailings until 1896 when she was disposed
of to London owners, who sold her on to
Sweden in 1897. She was one of barely a
dozen steamers built at Whitehaven, a
town which had a prodigious output of
coastal and deep-water sailing ships. Her
layout, with bridge amidships and engines
aft, is surprisingly modern-looking,
although her narrow funnel, sails and

slightly raking bow give away her true age.

MUNCASTER retained her original name
under Swedish ownership, but was
renamed ACHILEUS when sold to Greek
owners in 1914. On 5th August 1916 she
was sunk by gunfire from the German
submarine U 35 whilst passing Toulon.

SOUTHELLA (above)
J. Blumer and Co., Sunderland; 1875, 1,281gt, 242 feet
Seen amidst piles of timber, SOUTHELLA was interesting in several ways, not least in being owned by the same Hull company for 35 years. Jackson, Beaumont and Co. had her built and named after a nearby village, decorating her black funnel with two quite widely-spaced red bands. She was not sold until 1910, when renamed FINLAND TRADER by an owner in Abö - then under Russian domination and forced to fly their flag. Two years later she was sold to Sweden and renamed BELLGROVE, as which she was to return briefly to the British flag between 1917 and 1918. With unrestricted submarine warfare causing disastrous losses, The Shipping Controller used all sorts of means to obtain neutral ships, including invoking the powers of angary to exert the right of a belligerent to use neutral property. In some cases, this was done with the connivance of the owners, as under Swedish law it was illegal to sell a ship to a combatant during wartime. It is quite possible that the ageing BELLGROVE was idle in a British port - perhaps wanting spares - and the owners were not unhappy to receive some

compensation for her enforced UK service. They had her back in 1918, but BELLGROVE sank in November 1921, probably not far away from an appointment with the shipbreakers.

PLUTON (opposite page top)
James Laing, Sunderland; 1879, 1178gt, 225 feet
Another old steamer approaches Hull docks with what must be the ultimate in timber deck cargoes. Almost inevitably for a tramp of her period, PLUTON was British-built. She had begun life in Cardiff ownership as ACTIVITY, spending most of her career under the British flag in the fleet of the Gueret family who, like so many of Cardiff's shipowners, were incomers, probably from France. In 1900 the Guerets passed her on to owners in Rouen, who renamed her PLUTON, as seen here, although it is difficult to decide which of a series of French owners had her at the time: most likely it was Compagnie Brestoise de Navigation. In 1922 PLUTON became the Italian SENIO and achieved the not inconsiderable feat of surviving the Second World War. In 1948 she was rewarded for this by being renamed MAESTRALE, a singularly inappropriate

name for a ship which, if registers are to be believed, was still plodding along with the two-cylinder compound engines with which she first saw the light of the Sunderland day back in 1879. MAESTRALE survived until 1955 when breakers at Savona put an end to another remarkably long career.

MOUNT LEBANON (opposite page bottom)
A. Stephen and Sons, Glasgow; 1881, 2,420gt, 320 feet
With a fine counter stern and steam escaping from a tall funnel, MOUNT LEBANON looks her age: an example of the earlier British deep-sea tramp. Her canny Glaswegian owners have not wasted too much money on unneccesary fittings, and the two stump masts should be noted - the after one very stumpy indeed. Original owners were Smith and Service, and she moved on without change of name to John Bruce & Co. and W.S. Miller & Co., both of Glasgow. Fittingly, for a Clyde-owned and built steamer, Glasgow was the last port she visited. On a voyage to Alexandria with general cargo she foundered seventy miles west of the Scillies on 29th August 1908.

ANNIE (top)

William Gray and Co. Ltd., West Hartlepool; 1883, 1,651gt, 259 feet

Although *Lloyd's Registers* for the 1900s are awash with steamers named ANNIE, the letter Z visible on her funnel allows this one to be identified as being owned by Zerssen and Co. of Germany. Built as ERATO for Gladstone and Cornforth of West Hartlepool, she hoisted the German flag and became ANNIE in February 1896. In 1910 she was sold to Norwegian owners and renamed SKAGERAK. Her end came on 15th December 1917 in a collision with an unknown steamer off Grimsby whilst on a voyage from Bilbao to the Tees with iron ore.

HUBBUCK (bottom and opposite page)

J.L. Thompson and Sons, Sunderland; 1886, 2,834gt, 325 feet

HUBBUCK was built for William Lund of London, known for his Blue Anchor Line and the unfortunate WARATAH. HUBBUCK was employed on a UK to Australia service, offering limited accommodation for saloon passengers and very basic facilities for emigrants. The disposition of her masts, with one ahead of the funnel and two abaft, is unusual and may result from HUBBUCK having being fully rigged when new. Also of note are the white structures which look like lighthouses on either side of the forecastle: what are they?

The funnel colours - red with black top - indicate that the photograph was taken between 1898 and 1910 when HUBBUCK was owned by a company managed by T. Bowen Rees and Co., probably the Egypt and Levant Steam Ship Co. Ltd. based at Smyrna, now Izmir, in Turkey.

HUBBUCK passed to the Admiralty in 1915, although what use they made of her is uncertain: she was too good for a blockship but rather old for a transport. After this she could still find a buyer, however, and in 1920 went to owners in Valencia, Spain as EUGENIO DUTRUS. Just after her fortieth birthday, on 26th April 1926, she was wrecked near Tarifa, Spain.

JESSIE (top)

William Gray and Co. Ltd., West Hartlepool;
1891, 2,256gt, 281 feet

JESSIE had the simplest career of the ships pictured here. She was built and engined by Grays at West Hartlepool for Jens Nielsen, one of several German and Danish shipowners who settled in the town and gave rise to jokes about 'British West Hartlepool.' JESSIE remained with this owner and his son until 16th June 1917 when torpedoed and sunk by the German submarine U 82 about 260 miles south west of Bishop Rock. She was on a voyage from Alexandria to Hull with a cargo of cotton seed.

A feature of JESSIE's otherwise unremarkable appearance is the white structure mounted centrally on the bridge: the editors welcome suggestions as to its function.

SEVERUS (bottom)

William Gray and Co. Ltd., West Hartlepool;
1894, 3,409gt, 330 feet

The full set of yards and rigging on her foremast plus a very tall funnel suggests the SEVERUS is much older than she looks, but Abert's monumental work on German ships maintains that the only steamer of this name was built by Grays in 1894. Original owners were C. Andersen of Hamburg, whose markings are seen to remarkably good effect in the photograph: yellow funnel with narrow black band and red Maltese cross, plus red and white striped flag with white initials and four stars on a blue diamond.

Andersen was unlucky, or unwise, enough to charter SEVERUS to Russia in order to carry coal from Cardiff to Vladivostok at the time of the Russo-Japanese war, and on 24th February 1902 she was captured by the Japanese auxiliary HONGKONG MARU and taken to Japan. Here she was condemned as a prize, and renamed SHIBETORO MARU, later passing from the navy to Osaka Shosen K.K. Her adventures ended on 9th February 1918 when she stranded and sank south of Formosa whilst on a voyage from Sourabaya to Kobe with foodstuffs and general cargo.

THE PORT OF BARROW-IN-FURNESS
Part Two
Edward Paget-Tomlinson

Shipbuilding

Parallel with concern over the future of the port was the worry that the young shipbuilding industry was not healthy. James Ramsden entertained ideas for shipyards at the same time as he dreamt of docks, and his visions took a practical turn when in 1871 he met the Duke of Devonshire, James Little, and the Port Glasgow shipbuilder Robert Duncan, to establish the Barrow Shipbuilding Company at the same time as the Eastern Steamship Company. The first ship launched was the steam yacht ARIES (a modest 145gt) built for Sir James Ramsden; followed by five ships for the Eastern Steamship Company, although from the shipyard list it looks as if only three were ever launched. Vessels were built for the Anchor Line and its associated Barrow Steamship Company. The first naval order came in 1876 for the gunboat, FOXHOUND, but the yard did not prosper. Suffering from the general depression of the mid-1870s and plagued by strikes, the company had to be rescued by the Duke of Devonshire with a massive injection of cash. Later came the embarrassment of the Inman liner, CITY OF ROME (8,144/1881). She was designed to capture the Transatlantic speed record but failed to come up to expectations and Inman Line returned her to the builders with a considerable compensation claim. They transferred her to the still extant Barrow Steamship Company, and the Anchor Line took over her running although the latter never owned her. Eventually, after much modification, she proved quite successful and remained in service until 1902.

Salvation for the shipyard came in 1888 from Thorsten Nordenfelt and his submarines: from that time onwards the building of this type of naval vessel has been a regular task for Barrow's shipbuilders. Today, the specialist skills which they have developed has resulted in the construction of submarines of ever increasing size and sophistication. A new group, the Naval Construction and Armaments Company, was formed to take over the business and concentrate on the naval work. In spite of this much of its output was for the mercantile marine companies such as Pacific Steam, Canadian Pacific and Elder Dempster. But from 1894 naval work predominated: the first large warship built was the cruiser POWERFUL which was launched in 1895 and marked a milestone in Barrow's shipbuilding history.

This is not the place to expand on the rise and might of Barrow shipbuilding, but in 1896-7 the yard was taken over by Vickers, the Sheffield steelmakers.

HM Submarine B8 at Barrow in 1906. Vickers built all eleven boats of this class, and most of the Royal Navy's early boats; indeed Chatham Dockyard was the only other builder of British submarines until the First World War. The chimneys of the iron works are in the distance and a grain silo is seen to the right. *[Ken Royall collection]*.

This acquisition roughly parallels both the take-over of the Clydebank yard of J. & G. Thomson by the steelmakers, John Brown in 1899, and the interest shown in Laird's of Birkenhead by Charles Cammell of Sheffield from 1903. The expansion of the shipyard had altered the pattern of the docks at Barrow from an early date. Engravings show the west side of the Devonshire Dock as a fitting-out berth in the days of the Barrow Shipbuilding Company, a berth first expanded by the Naval Construction and Armaments Company and then extended again by Vickers to include the west side of the Buccleuch Dock. Timber yards gave way to machine shops and to cranes of increasing capacity, with Vickers buying the west side of the Devonshire Dock in 1900 and the west side of the Buccleuch in 1907. At about the same time the swing bridge crossing the waterway between the Buccleuch and Ramsden Docks was replaced by a rolling lift bascule bridge, and the opening was increased to 100 feet to accommodate the large warships being built. Later this widened opening was of immense benefit to the Cunard, P&O and Orient liners which were completed at Barrow. The east side of the Devonshire Dock remained a berth for the grain ships coming to Walmsley & Smith's flour mills, traffic which began in 1871 and continued until 1967. Ramsden Dock was equipped with hydraulic cranes and handled the ore imports needed by the Hindpool steelworks as local supplies became exhausted.

Shipbreaking

Shipbreaking was a later arrival on the scene. In October 1920 Thomas W. Ward Ltd. began to dismantle HMS ILLUSTRIOUS using a wharf at the entrance to the branch dock within Ramsden Dock – this vessel is seen in the aerial view in the first part of this article on page 84. Later, Wards expanded to occupy a site at the north eastern end of Devonshire Dock and to a berth just outside the dock entrance where final demolition of hulls took place.

Over the years many ships have been scrapped at Barrow, ranging from tugs and trawlers to large

Ships under repair in Devonshire Dock around 1900 (left). *Ken Norman collection.*

A smoky photograph of the Barrow-built SCYTHIA (19,930/1920) (below). She is attended by what must be the port's full complement of tugs, including the twin-funnelled, twin-screw FURNESS (225/1898) and CARTMEL (304/1907), plus WALNEY (185/1904). Because of a joiner's strike at Vickers, SCYTHIA was sent to Lorient to complete fitting out, and leaving Barrow she does indeed look not quite ready for service, with her white paintwork grimy from the yard. Despite the inauspicious start to her career, SCYTHIA gave Cunard remarkable service, 38 years of it. She was broken up at Inverkeithing in 1958. *[Sankey Collection 1975]*

Owned throughout her life by Bibby Line Ltd., the Harland & Wolff-built SOMERSETSHIRE (9,787/1921) came to Barrow to be broken up on 4th March 1954. Soon after the liner arrived, Ken Royall went to the docks hoping for a photograph of the complete ship. However, demolition had started immediately on arrival and already her foremast had been felled. [Ken Royall]

Built by John Brown & Co. Ltd. at Clydebank, the cruiser HMAS AUSTRALIA (9,870disp/1927) arrived at Barrow for breaking up on 5th July 1955. She had made an epic journey, towed by the Dutch tug RODE ZEE (500/1949) from Sydney, assisted by OOSTZEE (497/1953) from the Indian Ocean. For docking she has been handed over to one of Fisher's tugs, FISHERSHILL (292/1946) or FISHERSTOWN (232/1944). [Ken Royall]

liners. A number of former railway steamers finished up at Barrow, including GALTEE MORE (1,112/1898) PRAGUE (4,220/1930) and HIBERNIA (3,467/1920). Notable liners included P&O's BENDIGO (12,972/1922), scrapped at the tender age of 14 years, Canadian Pacific's veteran EMPRESS OF RUSSIA (16,810/1913), broken up in 1946 after being burnt out whilst refitting, and the MORETON BAY (14,376/1921) in 1957. Many naval vessels have also been dealt with. HMS ILLUSTRIOUS was followed by a former foe, the German battleship WESTFALEN which, after being stripped at Birkenhead, was broken up at Barrow in 1922. The monitor HMS ABERCROMBIE came to Barrow as did the cruisers HMS LONDON, HMS SCYLLA, HMS DIDO, and HMAS AUSTRALIA, towed from Sydney, Australia in three and a half months in 1955. HM Submarine EXCALIBUR, which arrived in February 1970, was intended to be the last vessel to be handled by Wards at Barrow but the yard was briefly reopened in 1972 to break up the Workington dredgers OLD SIDE (436/1908) and MOSS BAY (434/1901).

Ward's closure did not mean the end of shipbreaking at Barrow, however. In September 1972 the destroyer depot ship HMS TYNE arrived to be broken up by H Kitson Vickers & Sons (Engineers) Ltd. who also demolished two fleet minesweepers before moving their business to Fleetwood.

James Fisher & Sons plc

In contrast with the Eastern Steamship Company and the Barrow Steamship Company which were neither very successful, Barrow is the home of James Fisher & Sons plc, a shipping company which has developed out of all recognition. Founded in 1847 with a fleet of topsail schooners, by 1863 the company had 70 ships and peaked at 80 in 1878. In 1868 Fisher bought out Rawlinson's fleet of eight schooners and with them their shipyard at Barrow. This became the Furness Shipbuilding Company but it built only two schooners, both for Fishers. The company also had considerable mining interests in Northern Ireland and was responsible for building Fishertown, now known as Cargan. Steamers were introduced in 1883 with the SEA FISHER (297/1883) and there were seven in the fleet by 1908. On the outbreak of the First World War, Fishers had seven steamers and fourteen sailing vessels. Their first motor vessel was the Barrow-built SHOAL FISHER (698/1937) and by the Second World War the fleet comprised three motor vessels and seven steamers. The company has engaged in a wide variety of coasting and short-sea trades, not only the import of ore to Barrow and other local ironworks at Ulverston and Millom, but also further afield. They took vegetables into Weymouth, shipped containers to Belfast, and loaded gun turrets and other large fabrications at the Barrow shipyard. For the last-named trade they employed ships with long wide hatches incorporating bulged-out coamings.

Post-war years have seen many developments. The ABERTHAW FISHER (2,355/1966) and KINGSNORTH FISHER (2,355/1966) came into service in 1966, owned by Fishers and on long term charter to the Central Electricity Generating Board for the movement of heavy electrical equipment around the coast and occasionally overseas. In 1965 the company started handling the unique needs of British Nuclear Fuels Ltd. The STREAM FISHER (746/1943) was refitted for this trade and made her first voyage as such to Anzio in Italy. Later the LEVEN FISHER (1,540/1962) was adapted and voyaged regularly to Japan. The first ship specially-designed for this traffic was the PACIFIC SWAN

Fisher's LEVEN FISHER (1,540/1962), seen here arriving at Preston with a cargo of containers and Lancashire flats, was later converted for the carriage of irradiated nuclear fuel. In 1982 she was sold and renamed HAJ HASSAN, in 1989 became ALLAH KAREEM, and in 1994 DOJA, all under the Syrian flag. She is still listed in *Lloyd's Register* but no owners are recorded.

(4,527/1979), owned by Pacific Nuclear Transport Ltd. and managed by Fishers. She was the forerunner of a series of irradiated nuclear fuel carriers. Anchorage Ferrying Services Ltd. was jointly set up in 1968 for offshore lightening of bulk carriers bringing phosphate to Whitehaven. This was only one of a number of joint ventures with other local companies. 1978 saw Fisher's first involvement with passenger ships when the DARNIA (2,807/1977) was bought and chartered to Sealink and Manx Line, with their MANX VIKING (3,589/76), was taken over. More recent acquisitions have included Shamrock Shipping Co. Ltd. in 1981, Onesimus Dorey Ltd. in 1983, and Coe Metcalf Shipping Ltd. in 1984. Perhaps the biggest coup was acquiring the fleet of P&O Tankships Ltd. in 1997.

Today the activities of the company are many and diverse. Further tankers are being added to the fleet and are currently in production at Barrow. The first of these, the THAMES FISHER, had the distinction of being the first commercial vessel 'launched' into Devonshire Dock by means of the ship lift of VSEL's Devonshire Dock Build Hall. The Hall is at the northern end of the dock, which was in-filled in the early 1980s to accommodate it. Ironically, the dock was filled by dredging up material from Morecambe Bay which was pumped for several miles overland along a specially constructed pipeline to be deposited into the dock. This was a complete reversal of the never-ending and costly dredging of tidal silt which over the years was one of the reasons why the port never reached its expectations. Some of the spoil, which was originally removed, may have found its way back.

Barrow in the twentieth century

In 1923 under the railway grouping the Furness Railway Company gave way to the London, Midland & Scottish Railway Company as owners of the port. In the last days of the Furness Railway Company there had been improvements such as the lowering of the sill of the entrance lock to Ramsden Dock in 1916, and the replacement of the bridge across the Devonshire Dock entrance at the north end by a caisson. However, the depression of the inter-war years discouraged further work at Barrow. By the 1930s Barrow had some 12,000 feet of quayage and

The QUERNMORE (3,787/1923) was one of the few ships to operate a deep sea liner service out of Barrow in the twentieth century. She was owned by Furness sinsidiary Johnston Line Ltd., which became Johnston Warren Lines Ltd. in 1934. [Furness Museum]

Against the odds, merchant shipbuilding resumed at Barrow in the 1990s, and most fittingly it was on behalf of the town's most celebrated shipowner, James Fisher. Above, the tanker THAMES FISHER is rolled out of VSEL's Devonshire Dock Build Hall in 1997. [VSEL]

170,000 square feet of warehousing. In 1937, 757,138 registered tons of shipping used the port. An echo of the Anchor Line past was a service run by Furness Withy to New York started in the 1920s. This was operated by two ships DROMORE (4,096/1920) and QUERNMORE (3,787/1923) but this cargo-only service was not resumed after the Second World War.

The post-war history of Barrow is a tale of decline: although the shipyard was busy, the docks suffered from the run-down of other local industries. The Hindpool steelworks closed in 1963, followed by the Millom iron and steelworks in 1968. This meant an end to ore imports and the export of rails and foundry products. The end came for the no longer needed docks rail line when the Buccleuch Dock lifting bridge closed in 1966. It had become unsafe and was dismantled the following year. However, between 1969 and 1973 Barrow benefited from labour disputes at other ports and handled more general

An aerial view of Ramsden Dock Lock and the Anchor Line Basin on 13th August 1945. The war having just finished, Ward's quay has four destroyers alongside for breaking up. The lock contains a dredger, two hoppers and a tug. An ore ship unloads in Ramsden Dock, and two ocean-going ships are moored in the lock basin. Opposite them are three coasters probably loading coal from railway wagons.

cargoes such as cars, bananas, and other fruit. Containers came too, when Manchester Liners diverted their Great Lakes service to Barrow, and in 1969 Irish Ferries were operating from Barrow instead of Preston. In 1972 the original paper mill at Barrow closed, but Bowater Scott had opened another mill in 1967. This brought considerable wood pulp trade to Barrow for their large scale manufacture of tissues. However, they then began to import the pulp in ships that were too large to enter the port.

Recent events and the future

After 1963 the port was in the hands of the British Transport Docks Board, the successor to the Docks & Inland Waterways Executive which had taken over after the nationalisation of the railways in 1948. After the artificial prosperity of the early 1970s, it was the sad task of the Board to announce the withdrawal of cargo handling services at the end of 1974. The cranes, by this time electric, were dismantled and the handling plant was sold, leaving the port to continue solely as the servant of the shipyard.

Yet it was not the end. In 1979 British Nuclear Fuels Ltd. came to the east side of Buccleuch Dock for the handling of their cargoes in association with Fishers, and in 1982 a rail-connected terminal was opened at Ramsden Dock, managed by Fishers. In 1983 the British Transport Docks Board was privatised to become Associated British Ports, which is the present authority at Barrow. A resurgence of traffic followed, starting with the export of limestone quarried at nearby Stainton, and then in 1986 the condensate loading facility was established at Ramsden Dock. Condensate comprises the liquid hydrocarbon by-products of gas, in this case gas from the Morecambe Bay Field, which has provided plenty of shipping activity in several ways. In 1993 equipment, which included sections of pipeline, was imported for the North Morecambe gas terminal, and in 1994 the port was used by McDermott E.T.P.M. as the base for loading out pipeline for Hamilton Oil plc's Liverpool Bay project. With its central position, Barrow is well suited to serve the offshore oil and gas industries, and as the offshore fields develop and activity in the

Iron ore remained an important import into Barrow until the iron and steel works closed in the 1960s. Unloading Swedish ore in 1956 is Ragnar Källstrom's steamer SALTARÖ (4,254/1936), a possibly unique view of a ship whose career was soon to come to an end nearby (above).

The ship was built by Grays at West Hartlepool as TORDENE, one of four long bridge-deck ships for Dene Ship Management Ltd. of London. Although essentially they were tramps, they had some frills: note the wooden bridge apron. Dene concentrated on boilers-on-deck types after the Second World War, and disposed of their older ships. In 1947 TORDENE was sold to Einar Rasmussen of Norway who renamed her POLYANA, and sold her on to Källstrom of Stockholm in 1955.

On 29th November 1956, SALTARÖ was approaching Barrow with a cargo of ore from Luleå when she went aground off Sheep Island in the Walney Channel. She quickly broke in two. The afterpart was salvaged and towed into Barrow 13th February 1957 and the cargo discharged. On 3rd May 1957 the remains shown below were handed over to Wards for breaking up. It had been intended to discharge and salvage the forepart, but this was abandoned. *[Top: author's collection; bottom: Ken Royall]*

area increases, it seems likely that the port will benefit.

The Trident building programme demanded a new entrance to Ramsden to accommodate the size of the submarine hulls, and this was completed in 1992. Along with this work went an intensive dredging programme for the entrance approaches, which was reminiscent of the extensive dredging activity in Furness and LMS days when the two bucket dredgers MYLES KENNEDY (413/1921) and PIEL (1,226/1927) were at work, and the twin-screwed PIEL was able to carry her own spoil. Dredging work was later put out to contract with the Westminster Dredging Company and others.

With a continuing shipbuilding programme, Barrow remains the largest shipyard in the United Kingdom

and alongside this enterprise the port will continue to have a role, as well as maintaining specialist cargo facilities for the gas and nuclear industries. Activity now centres largely on Ramsden Dock and the Anchor Line Basin, the latter now including a ro-ro terminal. Recently the port's proximity to the Lake District, a feature exploited by the Furness Railway at the turn of the century, has seen a resurgence – albeit only on a small scale as yet – of the tourist traffic which had ceased in September 1914. In 1995 the cruise vessel SILVER WIND included a visit to the Lake District in her itinerary, and docked at Barrow to allow passengers to disembark for their tour. Two further visits were planned for 1998. None of this was in the mind of Sir James Ramsden or the Duke of Devonshire, but they would nevertheless be impressed, and probably Alfred Aslett more so.

A superb portrait of the paddle tug WALNEY, built in 1904 and the second tug of the name to work at Barrow. She was built by J.P. Rennoldson at South Shields for the Furness Railway, and passed through ownership of the London, Midland and Scottish Railway (who transferred her to Troon in 1931) to British Railways, who had her broken up in 1951. WALNEY had a passenger saloon and, as mentioned in the first part of this article, took some Barrow to Fleetwood sailings in her early days. [Sankey Collection 514]

A small ship for builders Cammell Laird & Co. Ltd., the tug RAMSDEN (188/1934) was completed for the London, Midland & Scottish Railway. In 1968, by when owners were British Railways, she was transferred to Heysham. Her stay there was short, however and, after being laid-up for much of the time, and she was towed away to Briton Ferry for breaking up in March 1970. [Ken Royall]

The bucket dredger PIEL is seen working in the Walney Channel on 22nd May 1956 (below). Built by Ferguson Brothers, Port Glasgow, PIEL finished her days at Barrow where Wards broke her up in late 1963. [Ken E. Royall]

THE PALMERS OF BOSTON AND RINGASKIDDY
Part Two
Gerald Lewis

MAY FLOWER - probably the second of the name and built in 1889 - taking on passengers for a pleasure cruise around Cork Harbour.
[G. Lewis collection]

Fleet list

1. **MAY FLOWER** (1) 1887-1907 Wooden screw tug.
O.N. 93406 42g 25n 73.5 x 14.3 x 7.2 feet.
2-cyl. by F.J. Harker, Stockton-on-Tees; 16 HP.
7.1887: Completed by George Brown, Sculcoates, Hull for Frederick Palmer, Boston as MAY FLOWER.
7.9.1891: Owner became Frederick Palmer junior, Cork.
5.10.1907: Register closed after she had been broken up.

2. **MAY FLOWER** (2) 1889-1919 Wooden screw tug.
O.N. 93407 50g 14n 75.6 x16.2 x 7.5 feet.
C. 2-cyl. built by Plenty and Sons, Newbury in 1881; 30 HP.
8.1889: Completed by George Brown, Wilmongton, Hull for Mrs Fanny Palmer (Frederick Palmer, manager), Spike Island, County Cork as MAY FLOWER.
25.8.1919: Register closed after she had been broken up.

3. **PERSEVERANCE** 1903-1932 Wooden cargo vessel.
O.N. 113743 108g 46n 86.7 x 21 x 7.8 feet.
C. 2 cyl. by M. Pratt, Huddersfield; 32 HP, 8 knots.
7.1903: Built by Frederick Palmer, Ringaskiddy for his own account as PERSEVERANCE.
1.3.1910: Owner became Ralph Palmer, Ringaskiddy.
30.12.1932: Broken up.
25.11.1934: Register closed.

PERSEVERANCE was built in 1903 at Palmer's own yard at Ringaskiddy.
[G. Lewis collection]

4. **MINER** 1907-1929 Screw tug.
O.N. 113746 50g 1n 65.0 x 15.0 x 9.8 feet.
C. 2 cyl. by Vosper, Portsmouth; 25 HP.
1880: Built by the Barrow Shipbuilding Co. Ltd., Barrow-in-Furness for the War Office as MINER.
1907: Acquired by Ralph Palmer, Ringaskiddy.
19.3.1929: Registry closed, vessel broken up.

A tug believed to be the MINER. *[G. Lewis collection]*

ALEXANDRA in Cork Harbour. The remains of a wooden coastal vessel can be seen behind her, waiting to be broken up by Palmers on the foreshore at Ringaskiddy. *[Richard Palmer collection]*

5. ALEXANDRA 1907-1955 Iron cargo vessel
O.N. 72364 120g 62n 110.0 x 19.1 x 8.9 feet.
C. 2-cyl. by Day, Summers & Co., Northam, Southampton; 60 HP.
1908: C. 2-cyl. by Frederick Palmer, Cork; 30 HP.
1876: Built by Day, Summers & Co., Northam, Southampton (Yard No. 38) for the New Southampton Steam Towing Co. Ltd., Southampton as ALEXANDRA.
1885: Owners became Southampton, Isle of Wight & South of England Royal Mail Steam Packet Company Ltd., Southampton.
1897: Sold via Joseph Constant, London to John R. Pethwick, Plymouth.
1906: Acquired by R. A. Lister & Co. Ltd., Dursley, Gloucestershire.
1907: Acquired by Samuel Palmer, Ringaskiddy.
1908: Re-engined.
21.9.1955: Arrived at Dublin for breaking up by Hammond Lane Foundry Ltd.

6. SHARK 1912-1940 Iron trawler
O.N. 98294 159g 79n 103.0 x 20.7 x 10.7 feet.
T. 3-cyl. by Great Grimsby Co-operative Box & Fish Carrying Co. Ltd., Grimsby; 45 HP.
10.1891: Completed by the Great Grimsby Co-operative Box & Fish Carrying Co. Ltd., Grimsby for the Steam Trawling Co. of Boston Ltd. (William F. Beaumont,

manager), Boston as SHARK.
1897: Owners became the Boston Deep Sea Fishing & Ice Co. Ltd., Boston.
1912: Acquired by Frederick Palmer, Boston.
1925: Sold to Samuel Palmer, Ringaskiddy.
8.10.1940: Sold to Department of Defence, Dublin, Ireland and commissioned as a Public Armed Ship of the Marine and Coastwatching Service, classed as a mine planter (minelayer).
9.9.1952: Arrived at Passage West, County Cork to be broken up by Haulbowline Industries Ltd.

7. MORSECOCK 1922-1953 Iron and steel twin screw tug.
O.N. 78757 325g 120n 155.5 x 25.1 x 12.1 feet.
Two x C. 2-cyl. by Laird Brothers, Birkenhead; 220 HP.
1877: Built by Laird Brothers, Birkenhead for William B. Hill, Liverpool as STORM COCK.
1881: Chartered by the Government for service at Alexandria.
1882: Sold to the Admiralty.
1922: Acquired by Samuel R. & Richard F. Palmer, Ringaskiddy and renamed MORSECOCK.
24.10.1949: Sold to Haulbowline Industries Ltd., Passage West, County Cork.
1.1950: Breaking up began at Passage West.

SHARK has retrieved a large anchor from the bottom of Cork Harbour. The man in the bowler hat is Ralph Palmer. *[Richard Palmer collection]*

MORSECOCK acting as tender to a White Star liner: note the houseflag. *[G. Lewis collection]*

MORSECOCK leaving Cork on a pleasure trip. [Richard Palmer collection]

AN SAORSTAT leaving Queenstown, Cobh. She and MORSECOCK appeared on page 161 of
Record 3, a photograph which inspired this article. [G. Lewis collection]

The tender FAILTE in Cork Harbour with a good load of passengers. [Peter Thomas collection].

ROYAL IRIS (registered in Dublin) leaving Cork. [National Maritime Museum N36942]

8. **AN SAORSTAT** 1927-1941 Steel twin screw ferry
O.N. 113422 514g 212n 155.6 x 42.1 x 11.0 feet.
2 x T. 4-cyl. by John Jones & Son, Birkenhead; 242 NHP.
1900: Built by John Jones & Son, Birkenhead (Yard No. 164) for the Wallasey Urban District Council, Wallasey as ROSE.
1910: Owners became Wallasey Corporation, Wallasey.
1927: Acquired by Samuel Palmer, Ringaskiddy and renamed AN SAORSTAT.
1941: Sold to the British Iron and Steel Corporation (Salvage) Ltd. (Arthur H. Turner, manager), Glasgow and renamed BISCOSALVE. Much of her superstructure was removed to fit her new role as a crane ship.
1948: Sold to John Lee (Stewart and Partners, managers), Belfast.
24.2.1951: Arrived at Preston in tow of the FORAGER (244/1945) to be broken up by T.W. Ward Ltd.

9. **FAILTE** 1927-1941 Steel twin screw ferry
O.N. 113451 514g 212n 155.6 x 42.1 x 11.0 feet.
2 x T. 4-cyl. by John Jones & Son, Birkenhead; 242 NHP.
1901: Built by John Jones & Son, Birkenhead (Yard No. 165) for the Wallasey Urban District Council, Wallasey as LILY
1910: Owners became Wallasey Corporation, Wallasey.
1927: Acquired by Samuel Palmer, Ringaskiddy and renamed FAILTE.
1941: Sold to Haulbowline Industries Ltd. (A.O. Hill, manager), Passage West, Cork.
8.5.1943: Wrecked in a gale about one and a half miles west of Bunessan, Mull.

10. **ROYAL IRIS** 1932-1946 Steel twin screw ferry
O.N. 123971 491g 146n 152.0 x 40.6 x 11.2 feet.
Two x T. 3-cyl. by David Rollo & Sons, Liverpool; 217 NHP.
5.1906: Completed by R. Stephenson & Co. Ltd., Hebburn-on-Tyne (Yard No. 100) for the Wallasey Urban District Council, Wallasey as IRIS.
1910: Owners became Wallasey Corporation, Wallasey.
1918: Requisitioned by The Admiralty and fitted out as an assault ship for the raid on Zeebrugge, where she was badly damaged but returned.
1919: Refitted for commercial service and renamed ROYAL IRIS.
1932: Acquired by Samuel R. & Richard F. Palmer, Ringaskiddy for use at Dublin.
1937: Used as a tender at Cork.
1946: Sold to Cork Harbour Commissioners, Cork and renamed BLARNEY.
13.12.1961: Breaking up began by Haulbowline Industries Ltd., Passage West, Cork.

11. **DURAS** 1921-1929 Iron auxiliary motor ship
O.N. 71844 117g 56n 95.9 x 18.1 x 9.7 feet.
C. 2 cyl. by J.P. Rennoldson & Sons, South Shields; 42 RHP, 10½ knots.
1921: Oil engine 6-cyl. 4SCSA built by Peter Brotherhood, Peterborough in 1917.
1924: Oil engine 2-cyl. DA built by Steijaard & Jannette Walen, Rotterdam, Holland in 1918; 90 BHP, 7½ knots.
1939: Oil engine 3-cyl. 4SCSA by Allen, Sons & Co., Bedford.
1.1893: Completed by J.P. Rennoldson & Sons, South Shields for the Galway Bay Steamboat Co. Ltd., Galway as DURAS.
10.1.1921: Acquired by Frederick Palmer junior, Boston and rebuilt as an auxiliary motor vessel.
1924: Re-engined.
6.9.1929: Sold to William C. Halliday (George Halliday, manager), Palnackie, Dalbeattie, Kirkcudbright.
29.5.1933: Sold to John Storm, Findhorn, Morayshire.
2.10.1933: Sold to John McConkey, Carrickfergus.
14.12.1936: Sold to W. & A. McMullan Ltd., Portaferry and William A. Glenn, Portavogie, County Down.
1939: Re-engined.
24.10.1942: Sold to William G. Garside, Oldham. Lancashire.
1.1947: Sold to Aage Jensen, Lemvig, Denmark and renamed STEEN B.
1951: Sold to H.S.A. Jensen, Copenhagen, Denmark.
1954: Deleted from *Lloyd's Register* due to lack of information.

S.S. DURAS. GALWAY. 4082. W.L.

DURAS is seen here as built: she was originally a steamer serving the Aran Islands from Galway and Ballyvaughan. Palmer bought her in 1921 and converted her to an auxiliary motorship, which would have altered her appearance drastically. Unfortunately, no photographs of the rebuilt DURAS have been located: can any reader help? *[National Library of Ireland]*

PUTTING THE RECORD STRAIGHT

Letters, additions, amendments and photographs relating to articles in any issues of *Record* are welcomed. Letters may be lightly edited.

AURIS revisited

Record 5, on pages 24-26, mentions Anglo-Saxon's AURIS and her gas turbine. The article quite correctly says that AURIS was built with four diesel-alternators connected to a single electric motor driving the propeller shaft. In August 1951 one of the four diesel alternators was removed and replaced with a gas turbine of the same power. AURIS then had three diesel alternators and one gas turbine alternator driving the single electric motor. After trials she sailed from Hebburn in October 1951 for Port Arthur, Texas, and made the voyage at an average speed of 9.21 knots compared with her original maximum speed of 12.85 knots. In March 1952 she crossed the Atlantic using the gas turbine alternator alone, possibly not planned, but because the three original diesel alternators were proving quite troublesome and all broke down!

What the article does not make quite clear is the next stage of the conversion work. By 1955 the operating results of this combination machinery had proved satisfactory, but it was decided to develop things to another stage. One of the 18,000 dwt. H-class newbuildings (HEMISINUS) was to have been fitted with two British Thomson-Houston gas turbo-alternators, basically a bigger version of the original machinery for the AURIS project. However, later advances meant that it became possible to use a gas turbine to directly drive the propeller shaft, and it was decided that it would best be installed as an experiment, so that more development work could be carried out. HEMISINUS was thus completed as a normal steam turbine tanker, and one of the gas turbines ordered was modified for direct drive, and installed in AURIS instead. Some reports suggest that the two gas turbines were intended for HEMIGLYPTA, but HEMISINUS was, in fact, the intended recipient.

The four alternators were removed and the main propulsion machinery replaced by a large single gas turbine of 5,300 bhp as the only means of propulsion. On trials the new gas turbine performed well, and the maximum speed of AURIS increased to 14.3 knots.

AURIS spent a considerable time under conversion at Cammell Lairds, Birkenhead from October 1956, partly because of industrial problems at the yard. Installation of the gas turbine was not completed until July 1958, and the project was not helped when AURIS suffered propeller damage on 22nd November 1958 by contacting a berth or lock wall whilst doing basin trials or shifting berth. The tanker left for sea trials in April 1959, but once again labour disputes delayed her entry into service until August 1959. Her successful operation in service was limited to six months. AURIS arrived in the Tyne from Rotterdam on 9th March 1960, and was still there in June, before being laid up in the River Blackwater for commercial rather than technical reasons. The Suez crisis of 1956 resulted in a thriving tanker market for a while as extra tonnage was needed. But the collapse of this market after United Nations salvage teams re-opened the canal on 9th April 1957 led to tanker rates reaching record lows, and many tankers were idle. Laid up in the River Blackwater at varying times were Shell's BATISSA, ERODONA, GALEOMMA, HELICINA, HYALINA, LATIA, LEPTON, LAMPANIA, LATIRUS, LIMATULA, LINGULA, NACELLA, NEOTHYRIS, NUCULANA,

PALUDINA, TENAGODUS and THALAMUS. Skyfotos/Fotoflite have a superb aerial photo showing 29 ships laid up in the Blackwater about 1958/59, which I think would be very interesting in *Record*.

The hull of AURIS was virtually a pre-1939 design, and during the three years of her conversion the size of tankers leapt from 28,000 dwt to 65,000 dwt or more, so that even a tanker of 18,000 dwt. was becoming small.

The conversion work resulted in some visible external alterations to the funnel, and these are clearly visible in one of the photos of her laid up in the River Blackwater. The engine casing was extended above the boat deck to accommodate the top of the heat exchanger and the waste heat unit. Prominent was the blow-off valve forward of the funnel and the uptake for the auxiliary boiler between the two after-supply fans.

AURIS arrived at Blyth on 5th August 1962 for demolition by Hughes Bolckow Ltd. on behalf of BISCO.
Captain MICHAEL PRYCE, 123B Westchester Drive, Churton Park, Wellington 6004, New Zealand.

Electric WINKLER

I was interested to read Alan McClelland's article on diesel-electric propulsion in *Record 5* and particularly his reference to the two tankers, BRUNSWICK and PERMIAN. It brought to mind memories of a similar, slightly smaller vessel owned by the Atlantic Oil Shipping Company, a subsidiary of the Atlantic Refining Company. This was the WINKLER (6,927/1930) built by Scott's Shipbuilding & Engineering Co. Ltd., Greenock and fitted with the same type of diesel-electric machinery as the two larger vessels. She had a similar cluster of exhaust pipes instead of a conventional funnel, and was Panamanian-registered. The WINKLER was a fairly regular visitor to the Mersey in the late 1930s, discharging part of her oil cargo into the tanks of the Liverpool Storage Company Ltd. in the West Float, Birkenhead and then proceeding up the Manchester Ship Canal to the Barton or Weaste Oil Wharf to discharge the remainder. She did not survive the war, being hit by torpedo from U 628 on 23rd February 1943 and sunk by gunfire from U 223 later the same day. I never managed to obtain a photograph of her, but the picture of this vessel in my mind's eye is as clear today as it was in 1938-39.

Congratulations on the continued high standard of *Record*, it is a first-class publication.
CRAIG J.M. CARTER, 15 King's Court, Well Lane, Higher Bebington, Wirral, Merseyside L63 8QL.

Forde and Fullagars

The comment about Guinness ships and the Second World War in *Record 6* reminds me of Frank Forde in *The Long Watch*, who noted the way ships were registered in Britain and Eire. It seems owners had not noticed the changed politics: from 1922 dominion status to republic in 1937, and carried on as previously flying the Red Ensign. It was war in 1939 that saw the Irish Tricolour hoisted and saw transfers of ships between the British and Irish registers, reflecting their true nationality.

Alan McClelland and John Hill both discuss the diesel-electric LA PLAYA of 1923 (*Record 5 and 6*). She was the first of three sisters built by Cammell Laird for United Fruit, all to be Fullagar-powered. The others were LA

The Skyfotos photograph of ships laid up in the River Blackwater during the late 1950s referred to in Michael Pryce's letter. Dry cargo ships are in the foreground (including at least two Liberty types) with tankers - mainly Shell-owned - in the background. *[Fotoflite incorporating Skyfotos]*

MAREA (3,689/1924) and LA PERLA (3,679/1925). LA MAREA was completed in this guise, but in 1930 was converted into a steam turbo-electric vessel with a British Thomson-Houston turbine powering a generator. Experience with these two and their engines saw LA PERLA completed as a steamer, powered by a Cammell Laird triple-expansion engine.

Fullagars had not been good news, only FLORIDA MARU (5,845/1925) and CUBA MARU (5,950/1926) survived past 1930 with these engines. The others had all been re-engined: FULLAGAR (420/1924), MALIA (3,872/1921), BARON DALMENY (3,496/1924), BRITISH AVIATOR (6,998/1924) and BRITISH CHEMIST (6,997/1925).

LA MAREA became DARIEN in 1930 and was broken up in 1954. LA PERLA had a long and varied life. Renamed CYGNUS in 1942 (USN storeship AF23), she reverted to LA PERLA in 1946. Sold in 1947 she carried the names LA PERLA I (1947), GIUBA (1949) and FRIGO ASIA (1957). My last note of her is under Brazilian ownership, out of commission in 1970.
DAVID BURRELL, 63 Avisyard Avenue, Cumnock, Ayshire KA18 3BJ.

Trunks on Tankers
I have just read 'Merits of the trunk' in *Record* 4, which has prompted this letter.

The trunk deck of Rowbotham's coastal tanker BRIDGEMAN (3,701/1972) is apparent as she approaches the locks at Eastham in 1975. Built at Aberdeen, the BRIDGEMAN was sold in 1994 by new owners P&O Tankships Ltd. and became SANDY.

In my 26 years at sea I have sailed in five different trunk deck tankers, the last being the chemical tanker ASTRAMAN (1,597/1973) in 1995 just prior to her sale abroad. Others were the product tankers BRIDGEMAN (3,701/1972) and HELMSMAN (3,705/1972), and the chemical tankers POLARISMAN (1,597/1973) and ORIONMAN (3,623/1975). All five belonged to Rowbotham Tankships Ltd. of London, which became P&O Tankships in 1993 and James Fisher Tankships in December 1996.

My own experiences of these trunk deck tankers during many voyages around the UK and Europe was that they were all well-found vessels and that the trunk decks were generally drier at sea than the main decks of other tankers. This must have contributed to their good safety record. They all served for more than 20 years before being sold on for further trading in various parts of the world.
Captain DW RICE, Sunset House, Flixton Park, Flixton, Bungay, Suffolk NR35 1NP

Three LANCINGs
In *Record 6*, page 107, LANCING is described as being commanded by an inspired captain, Nils Bull Melsom. At that time the owners were J. Johansen of Christiania, but

the LANCING was sold to Melsom & Melsom of Larvik about 1921 and was broken up in 1924 still as LANCING. I cannot help feeling that Captain Nils Bull Melsom had a part in the founding of Melsom & Melsom in 1919 and was involved in the purchase of LANCING from J. Johansen – possibly he recommended her purchase to the recently-established shipping line. Be that as it may, soon after LANCING was sold for demolition Melsom & Melsom built another ship and named her LANCING. By coincidence, this ship is shown on page 93 of *Record 6* as a whaling ship. Presumably, Melsom & Melsom's good experience with the sailing ship prompted them to use the name again for the whaling ship. As stated, the second LANCING lasted until she was torpedoed in 1942. But that was not the end of this saga, because Melsom & Melsom had yet another LANCING built for them, a 12,000 gross tons tanker delivered by Blythswood Shipbuilding Co. Ltd. in 1950. She remained with the company for ten years, when she was sold to Lundqvist Rederierna, Mariehamn without changing her name. Thus the third LANCING carried on for another 18 years before being broken up at Gijon. Like Melsom & Melsom, the Finnish owners must have regarded LANCING as a lucky name and were not prepared to change it.

Melsom & Melsom's tanker LANCING (11,957/1950), referred to in John B. Hill's letter. *[World Ship Photo Library collection]*

I hesitate to enter the discussion about split superstructures, save to recall that this arrangement was devised in the days of coal-burning steamships, when number three hatch was the bunker hatch. As is suggested, maintaining a separate bridge was probably due to 'old-established design practices'. But one wonders who was responsible for this attitude?

In my experience, when a new ship was contemplated, the design of the superstructure could have been the choice of:
  the shipyard
  the shipowner's board of directors
  the shipowner's naval architect (if they were big enough to employ one)
  the marine superintendent
  the engineer superintendent
In my view the most likely shipowners to maintain split superstructures were those in which the marine superintendent had the last word, or the ones who left such decisions to the builders.

I cannot see that effect on trim would be anything but marginal, bearing in mind today's practice is to put everything right aft. I might add that crane drivers and stevedores must have found it slower to manouevre cargo out of the ship when having to work between the bridge and the funnel.
JOHN B HILL, The Hollies, Wall, Hexham, Northumberland NE46 4EQ.

WENDOVER an eye-opener
Record 6 contains brilliant photographs and articles and once again brings back links with my own career at sea. One link with the past was with WENDOVER of Watts, Watts when I was second officer of NEW BROOKLYN of Elder Dempster Lines. WENDOVER was berthed close to us in the Royal Albert Dock, London around December 1950, and her officers gave us a conducted tour of their fine new ship. We were very impressed, and more so because our old NEW BROOKLYN had very limited accommodation and facilities. There was no hot and cold running water, and having a bath required two buckets of water obtained from the galley and cold water pump. One

bucket was to wash in, the other to be poured into a five-gallon empty drum with perforations which acted as a shower and was suspended from the deck head in the bathroom. Little wonder we were envious of the Watts, Watts officers. But having said all this, I was very happy in the NEW BROOKLYN and look back at her with affection – and believe it or not – she was ratted down in the foremast and mainmast shrouds.
Captain JOHN C. MORRIS, 5 Glen View Crescent, Heysham, Morecambe LA3 2QW.

I can remember way back in 1964 listening in awe to a young AB who had just come off one of the Watts, Watts ships describing the accommodation. We were at that time on an old Hains' tramp, our accommodation wrapped around the steering gear aft, with our cabin bulkheads ending a foot from the deckhead and finished off with chicken wire. Things did improve, but alas there are no ships now, although I'm still at sea albeit on the coast.
HC BAKER, 42 Princess Street, Perth PH2 8L5

No Dutch seizure
A small correction to the caption of HARPON on page 42 of *Record 5*: the SILESIA was not seized by the Dutch in Batavia 1914 – the Netherlands were strictly neutral. SILESIA was in East Asian waters in August 1914 when war broke out. She was laid up in the port of Batavia – Tandjong Priok – to avoid being captured by the Royal Navy. Her story involves the ill-fated Dutch Falmouth convoy. Seven Dutch steamers in convoy from Holland to various American ports to load food for the Dutch people, under the protection of the Dutch Government and with the permission of the Germans, had to enter Falmouth for inspection by the British. On their way to Falmouth all seven were torpedoed by the German submarine U 21. After prolonged negotiations the Germans granted that the seven steamers were torpedoed by mistake on that day, 22nd February 1917. Some German steamers, laid up in Indonesian waters and having more or less the same value, were handed over to the Dutch Government on 29th October 1918 as replacements. They received the same names as the torpedoed vessels: BANDOENG, EEMLAND, GAASTERLAND, JACATRA, NOORDERDIJK and

NEW BROOKLYN (6,546/1919), whose accommodation presented such a contrast to that of WENDOVER, served Elder Dempster particularly well, from 1920 through to 1954. John S. Latsis got a few more years' service out of the old steamer as MARIANNA until she was broken up at Spezia in 1959. *[World Ship Photo Library collection]*

ZAANDIJK (ex SILESIA). The seventh steamer in the convoy, MENADO, had reached a UK port, heavily damaged, and was therefore not replaced. After the Armistice, the Allies challenged the agreement between the Dutch and the Germans. After long negotiations, on 21st February 1920 it was agreed that the ZAANDIJK and others could sail for Holland.
MARTIN LINDENBORN, Postbus 5125, NL-6802, EC Arnhem, Netherlands.

Less than ILLUSTRIOUS
On page 84 of Record 6 *an aerial view of Barrow Docks showed what we assumed from its size was a cruiser being broken up by T.W. Ward Ltd. Bob Todd of the National Maritime Museum tells us that it is, in fact, the remains of the pre-Dreadnought HMS ILLUSTRIOUS, built at Chatham Dockyard in 1898 and sold to Wards for demolition after the First World War. Dr Ian Buxton confirms that she arrived in November 1920, and that Ward's next demolition at Barrow was the German battleship WESTFALEN, which arrived in May 1922. These dates, the amount of ILLUSTRIOUS left, and relatively short shadows suggests the photograph was taken in the summer of 1921.*

John Hill suggests that the freighter on the opposite berth is one of the N type standard ships built by Harland & Wolff during the First World War, eight of which were acquired by Elder, Dempster during 1919 and 1920. They were given names beginning NEW, for instance NEW BRIGHTON and NEW BROOKLYN, the latter illustrated on the previous page. The V-shaped transom stern which was a feature of these prefabricated ships can just be discerned in the aerial photograph.

Two flags, several suggestions

The photograph of BEGONIA flying two flags from her ensign staff in Record 6 *has prompted a number of suggestions as to when a ship might fly two national flags: namely, courtesy, capture or ceremony. But BEGONIA does not fit into any of these categories, and the usual position for flags on such occasions would be from a mast or stay. The closest parallel seems to be with German vessels in the years immediately after the Second World War which flew an international signal flag inferior to their national flag on the ensign post, presumably indicating that the occupying power had given them permission to trade. It is just possible that the BEGONIA's lower flag – thought to be the international code flag T – somehow indicated that Finland gave this Swedish-registered ship permission to trade under their flag, which appears to be the national flag being flown. A further possibility is that the lower flag is a local signal, possibly used on the Manchester Ship Canal. Does anyone with knowledge of Finnish or Swedish shipping, or the Mersey between the wars, recall such usage? Thanks to John B. Hill, Richard Cornish, Mike Cooper and Christopher Rickard. Editor.*

LOOSE ENDS:
GERMAN TRUNKS AND GUINNESS BARGES

We naively thought that the article on Swedish trunk deckers in *Record 5* was the last word on ships built to this design, intended partly to get round Doxford's patents on their hugely successful turret design, and which enjoyed a certain vogue in the Swedish ore trades. However, Harold Appleyard who compiled the original article and fleet list has found details of two further trunks built in Sunderland for Hamburg-Amerika Line. DORTMUND and HOERDE were completed by Laings – who had built the OSCAR II for Sweden five years earlier – after a German yard had constructed a further group for Swedish owners. The building of such ships by Hamburg-Amerika – essentially a passenger and cargo liner company – is interesting. The trade in Swedish iron ore, largely handled through Norwegian ports, was to be of considerable importance to a blockaded Germany in both world wars. Is it too fanciful to suggest that the German government had asked that the company should build ore carriers, perhaps in return for a mail subsidy for a Hapag liner?

DORTMUND
4,970g 3,228n 375.7 x 55.1 x 26.1 feet.
T. 3-cyl. by George Clark Ltd., Sunderland.
4.4.1901: Launched by Sir James Laing and Sons Ltd., Sunderland (Yard No. 583) for Hamburg-Amerika Packetfahrt A.G., Hamburg, Germany as DORTMUND.
25.6.1901: Completed.
7.8.1914: Seized at Nicolaiefsk by Russia. Transferred to the Russian Volunteer Fleet Association and renamed IRTYSH.
1922: Transferred to Arcos Ltd. (Russian Norwegian Navigation Co. Ltd., managers), London. Placed under the British flag and registered at Blyth although remaining under Soviet control.
5.6.1924: Sold to German shipbreakers.

HOERDE
4,974g 3,230n 375.9 x 55.1 x 26.1 feet.
T. 3-cyl. by George Clark Ltd., Sunderland.
21.5.1901: Launched by Sir James Laing and Sons Ltd., Sunderland (Yard No. 584) for Hamburg-Amerika Packetfahrt A.G., Hamburg, Germany as HOERDE.
10.8.1901: Completed.
7.6.1910: Sold to P. Brown junior & Co., Copenhagen, Denmark and renamed ATLANTIC.
15.6.1911: Sold to Hamburg-Amerika Packetfahrt A.G., Hamburg, Germany and renamed HOERDE.
7.1914: Fitted out as a collier at Manila.
31.8.1914: Sailed to carry out bunkering duties off Sumatra.
26.9.1914: Interned at Sabang.
9.10.1919: Surrendered to Great Britain as a war prize and allocated to The Shipping Controller (British India Steam Navigation Co. Ltd., managers), London.
1920: Sold to the Byron Steam Ship Co. Ltd. (M. Embiricos manager), London and renamed GENERAL MILNE.
10.1928: Sold to A.M. Milonas, Piraeus, Greece and renamed EVGENIA MILONA.
1934: M.A. Embiricos appointed manager and renamed AMVRAKIKOS.
3.5.1934: Arrived at Spezia to be broken up by Cantieri Santa Maria.

DORTMUND at Antwerp *[Peter Newall collection]*

The steam barges used to carry Guinness between the St. James' Gate Brewery and the Custom House Quay, and around Dublin were mentioned on page 67 of *Record 6*, where a photograph was reproduced to which had been added some fanciful depictions of these craft. Guinness began to run their own barges on the Liffey in 1868, the type depicted on the W.M. BARKLEY photograph being built around 1892 and named after Irish rivers. Replacement steamers were

built by the Liffey Dockyard between 1929 and 1931, and measured 80 feet and 80gt. Their names were taken from districts of Dublin or houses owned by the Guinness family: CASTLEKNOCK, CHAPELIZOD, CLONSILLA FERRYHOUSE, HOWTH, KILLINEY, KNOCKMAROON, SANDYFORD and SEAPOINT. The last was sold in 1961 when the Victoria Wharf at Guinness's brewery was demolished.

Laurence Dunn has very kindly loaned photographs of some of these little Guinness steamers which he took in 1958. In the upper photograph, SANDYFORD passes THE LADY GWENDOLEN. CLONSILLA (lower photograph) is carrying empty barrels judging by her draft. She is steaming past another barge which has the number 27 visible on her funnel, and is unloading barrels with her own derrick. *[Both: Laurence Dunn, with thanks to Terry O'Conalláin for information]*

EVERY PICTURE TELLS A STORY

It is 26th April 1947, and photographer John McRoberts records what could have been an embarrassing – and quite possibly worse – collision between the Blue Funnel Victory-type MEMNON (7,687/1945) and Cunard's MAURETANIA (35,677/1939) in the Mersey, witnessed by Rea's tug YORKGARTH (179/1922). Thanks to some urgent activity in MEMNON's engine room – note the smoke the steam turbine ship is emitting – disaster was averted. This fascinating photograph came to

light during picture research for the latest *Ships in Focus* publication, a pictorial history of Blue Funnel which we believe will be the most comprehensive ever compiled on this most famous company. At the risk of making this feature *Every picture plugs a book,* we would add that subscribers to *Record* can buy *Ships in Focus: Blue Funnel Line* at a concessionary price of £21 post free, a saving of £2.50. Details of how to order will be found inside the front cover.

SOURCES AND ACKNOWLEDGEMENTS

Photographs are from the collection of John Clarkson unless otherwise credited. We thank all who gave permission for their photographs to be used, and are particularly grateful to Peter Newall; David Whiteside and Tony Smith of the World Ship Photo Library; and to Ivor Rooke, George Scott and the museums and institutions listed for help in finding photographs.

In researching captions, sources have included the *Registers* of William Schell and Tony Starke, *Lloyd's Register, Lloyd's Confidential Index, Lloyd's War Losses, Mercantile Navy Lists,* and *Marine News.* Use of the facilities of the World Ship Society's Central Record, the Guildhall Library and Lloyd's Register of Shipping are gratefully acknowledged. Particular thanks also to William Schell and John Bartlett for information and to Heather Fenton for editorial services.

Dublin gas boats
Thanks to Pat Mullen, who sailed in the Gas Company steamers and motorships; Captain Frank Forde, author of *The Long Watch,* for details of war incidents and casualties; and correspondence with the company from an Irish priest in Burma whose interest in Irish ships must have helped sustain him so far from home.
Sullivan, CJO *The Gas Makers (Perspectives on the Irish Gas Industry)* Dublin 1987.
Roy Fenton produced the fleet list.

Port of Barrow-in-Furness
Many thanks to Captain J.W. Green, Port Manager, Associated British Ports, Barrow, Fleetwood and Silloth; Ken J. Norman of Barrow-in-Furness, and Nick Stanbra.

Printed sources were:
Associated British Ports. *Port of Barrow-in-Furness, 125th Anniversary 1867-1992.*
Associated British Ports. *Port of Barrow.* Current brochure.
Associated British Ports in association with the Furness Tourism Partnership. *The Port of Barrow. By Sea to the English Lakes.*
Various contributors. Furness Railway 150. Cumbrian Railways Association, 1996.
Green, JW. *The Port of Barrow.*
Hammersley AD. *The Port of Barrow-in-Furness.*
Haws, D. *Merchant Fleets No. 9, Anchor Line.* TCL Publications, Pembroke, 1986.
Marshall JD. *Furness and the Industrial Revolution.* Barrow-in-Furness, 1958.
Norman KJ. *Railway Heritage. The Furness Railway.* Silver Link Publishing, Peterborough, 1994.
Owen, D. *Ports of the United Kingdom.* Allman & Son, London, 1939.
Rothwell, C. Over the Sea to Lakeland. *Preview of Lakeland.*
Sankey, R. *Maritime Heritage. Barrow and Morecambe Bay.* Silver Link Publishing, Peterborough, 1986.
The credit for the photograph on page 78 of *Record 6* should have read G. Holme.

Antiques in the Humber
Thanks to Arthur Credland, Keeper of Maritime History at the Town Docks Museum, Hull for information on Marcus Barnard.

Whilst compiling this issue we were sorry to learn of the death, on 25th July, of Captain Ken Shaw, whose career was subject of an article in *Record 2*.